Llewellyn's 2012

Witches'
Spell-A-Day
Almanac

Holidays & Lore
Spells, Rituals & Meditations

Copyright 2011 Llewellyn Worldwide.
Editing: Sharon Leah; Interior Design: Michael Fallon & Sharon Leah
Cover Design: Lisa Novak
Background Photo: © PhotoDisc
Interior Art: © 2011, Steven McAfee
pp. 11, 31, 49, 69, 91, 109, 127, 147, 167, 185, 207, 231
Spell icons throughout: © 2011 Sherrie Thai
You can order Llewellyn books and annuals from *New Worlds*,
Llewellyn's catalog. To request a free copy of the catalog, call toll-free
1-877-NEW WRLD, or visit our website at www.llewellyn.com

7-12147

f Llewellyn Worldwide Ltd.
Drive
55125

D1302226

Table of Contents

About the Authors

Chandra Alexandre is an ititiated Tantrika and hereditary witch. The founder and executive director of SHARANYA (www.sharanya.org), Chandra has worked to help those in the West seeking to embrace the ancient (yet living) embodied and goddess-centered spiritual traditions of India. Chandra holds a PhD in philosophy and religion, and an MBA in sustainable management.

Elizabeth Barrette has been involved with the Pagan community for more than twenty years. She serves as the managing editor of *PanGaia* and the Dean of Studies at the Grey School of Wizardry. She lives in central Illinois and enjoys gardening for wildlife and stone magic. Visit her LiveJournal "The Wordsmith's Forge" at ysabetwordsmith.livejournal.com/

Deborah Blake is a Wiccan high priestess who has been leading Blue Moon Circle for many years. She is the author of *Everyday Witch A to Z: An Amusing, Inspiring & Informative Guide to the Wonderful World of Witchcraft*, *The Goddess in the Details: Wisdom for the Everyday Witch*, and *The Everyday Witch A to Z Spellbook*.

Boudica is reviews editor and co-owner of *The Wiccan/Pagan Times* and owner of *The Zodiac Bistro*, both online publications. A former New Yorker, she now resides with her husband and eight cats in Ohio.

Dallas Jennifer Cobb believes life is what you make it. Jennifer has made a magical life in a waterfront village on the shores of great Lake Ontario. She practices manifestation magic and wildlands witchcraft. She currently teaches pilates, works in a library, and writes to finance long hours spent following her heart's desire—time with family, in nature, and on the water. Contact her at jennifer.cobb@live.com.

Raven Digitalis is a Neopagan priest of the "disciplined eclectic" shadow magic tradition Opus Aima Obscuræ, and is a radio and club DJ. He is the author of *Goth Craft: The Magickal Side of Dark Culture*. With his priestess Estha, Raven holds community gatherings, tarot readings, and a variety of ritual services. The two also operate the metaphysical business Twigs and Brews.

Ellen Dugan, a.k.a. "The Garden Witch," is an award-winning author and a psychic-clairvoyant. She has been a practicing Witch for more than twenty-four years. Ellen has written many books, including *Garden Witchery*, *Cottage Witchery*, and *How to Enchant a Man*. Visit Ellen online at ellendugan.com.

Ember Grant is a freelance writer, poet, and regular contributor to Llewellyn's annuals. She lives in Missouri with her husband of thirteen years and their two feline companions.

Magenta Griffith has been a witch more than thirty years and a high priestess for more than twenty years. She is a founding member of the coven Prodea, which has been celebrating rituals since 1980. She is also a member of various Pagan organizations, such as Covenant of the Goddess. She presents classes and workshops at a variety of events around the Midwest. She shares her home with a small black cat and a large collection of books.

James Kambos is a regular contributor to Llewellyn annuals whose spell crafting spark began when he watched his grandmother create spells based on Greek folk magic. When not writing, he paints in the American primitive style. He calls the beautiful Appalachian hill country of southern Ohio home.

Mickie Mueller is award-winning artist of fantasy, fairy, and myth. She is an ordained Pagan minister and has studied natural magic, Celtic tradition, and Faerie Tradition. She is also a reiki healing master/teacher in the Usui Shiki Royoho Tradition. Mickie is the illustrator of *The Well Worn Path* and *The Hidden Path* decks and the writer/illustrator of *The Voice of the Trees, A Celtic Ogham Divination Oracle*.

Lee Obrien is a freelance writer and educator. He lives in St. Paul, Minnesota, where he enjoys walking when the weather is fair, gardening, reading, and spending time with his family and one feline friend.

Paniteowl has organized and presented at festivals and gatherings over the past two decades throughout the East Coast and Canada. She is founder of the Mystic Wicca Tradition and lives with her husband, Will, on a 56-acre woodlot in the mountains of northeast Pennsylvania, where they have hosted biannual gatherings for Pagans for the past fifteen years.

Susan Pesznecker lives in Oregon and teaches writing at Portland State University and Clackamas Community College. She also teaches an online course in magic through the Grey School of Wizardry.

Kelly Proudfoot, originally from Australia, now lives in Nashville, Tennessee, and is working on a self-help book about assessing and changing your life path through ritual, analysis, dream interpretation etc. She's been a practicing numerologist and tarot reader for twenty years, a solitary eclectic

Wiccan since 1996, and is interested in magical herbalism, mythology, dream therapy, and quantum mechanics. She is in the process of setting up her herb farm and Wiccan supplies business.

Tess Whitehurst is the author of *Magical Housekeeping: Simple Charms and Practical Tips for Creating a Harmonious Home* and *The Good Energy Book: Creating Harmony and Balance for Yourself and Your Home.* She's also an intuitive counselor, feng shui consultant, and columnist for *Witches and Pagans* magazine. Her website (www.tesswhitehurst.com) features simple rituals, meditations, and musings for everyday magical living. Tess lives in Venice Beach, California.

A Note on Magic and Spells

The spells in the *Witches' Spell-A-Day Almanac* evoke everyday magic designed to improve our lives and homes. You needn't be an expert on magic to follow these simple rites and spells; as you will see if you use these spells throughout the year, magic, once mastered, is easy to perform. The only advanced technique required of you is the art of visualization.

Visualization is an act of controlled imagination. If you can call up in your mind a picture of your best friend's face or a flag flapping in the breeze, you can visualize. In magic, visualizations are used to direct and control magical energies. Basically, the spell caster creates a visual image of the spell's desired goal, whether it be perfect health, a safe house, or a protected pet.

Visualization is the basis of all good spells, and as such it is a tool that should be properly used. Visualization must be real in the mind of the spell caster so that it allows him or her to raise, concentrate, and send forth energy to accomplish the spell.

Perhaps when visualizing you'll find that you're doing everything right, but you don't feel anything. This is common, for we haven't been trained to acknowledge—let alone utilize—our magical abilities. Keep practicing, however, for your spells can "take" even if you're not the most experienced natural magician.

You will notice also that many spells in this collection have a somewhat "light" tone. They are seemingly fun and frivolous, filled with rhyme and colloquial speech. This is not to diminish the seriousness of the purpose, but rather to create a relaxed atmosphere for the practitioner. Lightness of spirit helps focus energy; rhyme and common language help the spell caster remember the words and train the mind where it is needed. The intent of this magic is indeed very serious at times; and magic is never to be trifled with.

Even when your spells are effective, magic won't usually sparkle before your very eyes. The test of magic's success is time, not immediate eye-popping results. But you can feel magic's energy for yourself by rubbing your palms together briskly for ten seconds, then holding them a few inches apart. Sense the energy passing through them, the warm tingle in your palms. This is the power raised and used in magic. It comes from within and is perfectly natural.

Among the features of the *Witches' Spell-A-Day Almanac* are an easy-to-use "book of days" format; new spells specifically tailored for each day of the year (and its particular magical, astrological, and historical energies); and additional tips and lore for various days throughout the year—including color correspondences based on planetary influences, obscure and forgotten holidays and festivals, and an incense of the day to help you waft magical energies from the ether into your space.

In creating this product, we were inspired by the ancient almanac traditions and the layout of the classic nineteenth-century almanac *Chamber's Book of Days*, which is subtitled *A Miscellany of Popular Antiquities in Connection with the Calendar*. As you will see, our fifteen authors this year made history a theme of their spells, and we hope that by knowing something of the magic of past years we may make our current year all the better.

Enjoy your days, and have a magical year!

Spells at a Glance by Date and Category*

	Health	Protection	Money/ Success	Love	Clearing/ Cleaning	Relationship	Divination / Meditation
Jan.	18, 25		8, 13, 26	20	2, 12, 17	16, 24, 30	11, 14
Feb.	16, 27	3, 19		14	4, 23	17, 26	2, 22, 28
Mar.			29	1, 13	17	4, 23, 26	14, 19, 21
Apr.	10, 23	15, 21	7	3	18, 30		4, 11, 20, 26
May		10, 16, 29	24	8, 11, 25, 27	2	3	4, 9, 19, 23, 30
Jun.	10, 14	7, 15, 17, 23	21	1, 9	16	24	8
Jul.	24	2, 31	14	7		28	4, 6, 26
Aug.	7	2, 19	23		11, 18	6	4, 8, 16, 20
Sep.		1, 5, 12, 13, 18, 24, 26, 29	20	25	7, 28	6, 11, 21	17
Oct.		1, 16		19	6		13, 15, 18, 25, 26
Nov.	19	17, 20, 27	18	16, 24, 30		15	11
Dec.	15	20, 30	21, 31	12, 27, 29	11, 14	19	2, 7, 16, 25

* List is not comprehensive.

 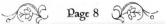

2012

Year of Spells

January

January is the first month of the year in the Gregorian calendar. On average, it is the coldest month in the Northern Hemisphere and the warmest month in the Southern Hemisphere. January is named after the Roman god Janus, the god of doorways. Janus is typically depicted with two faces, so he could see both what was behind him and what was in front of him. The side that faced the past was shown as mature and bearded, whereas the side that faced the future was youthful and full of hope. Janus's name came from the Latin word for door, *ianua*, and so January is the doorway into the new year. January is a quiet month after all the hustle and bustle of the holiday season. For those who follow the Wheel of the Year, it falls between Yule, when we celebrate the slow return of the light, and Imbolc, when we anticipate the first stirrings of spring. For many, it is a long, dark, cold month, but one that allows us to turn our focus inward, and to prepare for the journey that is the year to come. Like Janus, may we turn our faces forward with hope and youthful enthusiasm.

Deborah Blake

January 1
Sunday

New Year's Day – Kwanzaa ends

 1st ♈
2nd Quarter 1:15 am

Color of the day: Gold
Incense of the day: Juniper

Welcome the New Year

Today is a traditional day of new beginnings. Focus on a specific resolution if you like, or simply send out a request for a happy and prosperous year to come. Wrap equal amounts of the following dried herbs in a white cloth: lavender, rose petals, rosemary, thyme, and basil. Tie the bundle and chant:

> To bring me luck,
> To bring me love,
> for peace and to protect.
>
> May insight be
> a guide to me—
> no worries, no regrets.
>
> Success be mine,
> patience and time,
> I cast this New Year's spell.
>
> I now begin,
> with hope I send,
> a wish that all be well.

Carry this talisman with you or keep it on your altar as long as you like.

Ember Grant

January 2
Monday

 2nd ♈
☽ v/c 3:07 pm
☽ → ♉ 5:16 pm

Color of the day: Ivory
Incense of the day: Narcissus

An Ice Spell

While the year is still new, use this ice spell to rid yourself of any negativity. First light a gray candle to neutralize all negative forces you feel you should get rid of. Next, in a dark-colored bowl, place an odd number of ice cubes in the bowl—three, five, seven, or nine—and then fill the bowl half full with water. Use your power hand or athame to stir the ice cubes counterclockwise. Begin gently, then faster. Feel all the forces you wish to rid yourself of swirling away from you. Visualize your problems disappearing into the darkness of the bowl; "see" them being drawn away from you. When you feel the banishment is complete, stop stirring the ice and extinguish the candle. Leave the ice cubes alone and let them melt completely. Then pour the water down a drain, and as you do, feel the negativity going with it.

James Kambos

 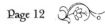

January 3
Tuesday

 2nd ♉

Color of the day: Scarlet
Incense of the day: Ginger

Smooth Transition Spell

Before resuming work after a good, long holiday, cast a quick Smooth Transition Spell. Stand in the kitchen in your bare feet. Visualize the Earth's energy flowing up and into you and affirm:

> I am grounded and level.
> I am strong and stable.

Breathe deeply, intoning:

> I am inspired, thought-filled,
> and light.

Run water into a tea kettle or coffee pot. Welcome the energy of Water by saying:

> Like this water, I flow easily,
> fluid and clear.

As the water heats, harness the power of Fire by saying:

> I am purified, cleansed, and
> filled with passion.

When your tea or coffee is ready, pour a cup and breathe in the aroma. Welcome the energy of Air and the blend of elements while saying:

> With these elements I face the
> day with ease and grace.
> So be it.

Now drink deeply.

Dallas Jennifer Cobb

NOTES:

January 4
Wednesday

2nd ♉

Color of the day: Topaz
Incense of the day: Bay laurel

Serenity

Everything is cold, the holiday hubbub has passed, and things are quieting down; does it seem a bit anticlimactic? We've spent the last two months surrounded by distractions of the holidays. This is the time that the world sleeps. If you take some time to visit nature right now, it's like looking at a sleeping baby—nothing else is so peaceful. Embrace the change of pace, bundle up, and take ten minutes or so to step outside somewhere—your yard, balcony, a park—and listen to nature sleep. Whisper this charm:

> As the world sleeps to this lullaby
>
> Reveal your mysteries, by and by.

See what happens. Watch for nature's signs of life during the Earth's wintery sleep. When you find them, they will reveal mysteries to you that you would have missed if you hadn't taken a little time to experience the serenity of this time of year.

Mickie Mueller

January 5
Thursday

2nd ♉

☽ v/c 3:46 am

☽ → ♊ 5:44 am

Color of the day: Crimson
Incense of the day: Nutmeg

Rowan Berries to Calm the Mind

The rowan tree is known for its mystical powers. Although the tree doesn't grow in all parts of the country or world, many witches make wands from its branches, which is one of its most popular uses in the magical arts. My favorite part of the tree is the berries, which are renowned for helping assimilate scattered energy. If your mind is overwhelmed or scattered, if you feel rushed or panicked, or if you need some instant grounding and centering, grab some rowan berries (I prefer them either in a cup or threaded as a necklace), slip into meditation, and visualize your scattered energy returning to your body and mind. You may wish to create an accompanying chant to assist with the energy work, such as "Energy returning, mind lifted, emotions grounded," or something similar. If you create a chant, you may choose to either repeat it out loud or in your head while performing the visualization.

Raven Digitalis

January 6
Friday

 2nd ♊

Color of the day: Purple
Incense of the day: Yarrow

Spell for happiness and Wisdom

La Befana flies through the skies on her broom and delivers fruit and gifts to children of Italy. When they wake up on the sixth of January, they see what treats Befana has left for them. Her associations include her broom, figs, dates, and honey. Befana is linked to Hecate and may be a deity of the ancestral spirits, the forest, and the passing of time. Today is when many traditions put away the trappings and trimmings from the winter holidays. Before you do the same, light a white candle for the waxing Moon and call on Befana to spread a just a little more holiday magic into the world.

> *La Befana the good witch of Italy, I call for your joy to quickly surround me.*
>
> *May your gifts bring happiness and wisdom true, may I be joyful in all things that I do.*

Ellen Dugan

January 7
Saturday

2nd ♊
☽ v/c 2:52 pm
☽ → ♋ 4:05 pm

Color of the day: Blue
Incense of the day: Sandalwood

Distaff Day

Distaff Day is a medieval holiday that concludes the Twelve Days of Christmas. A distaff is a stick or spindle used to draw out wool, cotton, or linen and spin it into thread. Spinning was women's work, and the term "spinster" represented an unmarried woman who spent her days doing mundane, necessary tasks. The blunt side of the distaff was considered "female," while the sharp side of the distaff was called the "spear," a phallic term representing the male aspect. In medieval times, household chores were put on hold throughout Yule, but once the festival ended, women picked up their distaffs and went back to work. Practice magic of hearth and home by placing a distaff or spindle on your altar: use it as a symbol of the God and Goddess, or inscribe with the Gebo rune and use it to meditate on the balanced relationship between hard work and celebration.

Susan Pesznecker

January 8
Sunday

2nd ♋

Color of the day: Amber
Incense of the day: Almond

Success Spell

As you work into the New Year, following your resolutions can seem overwhelming. Doing a spell of success and purification will help you keep your resolutions by eliminating obstacles.

Get out your Book of Shadows, where you wrote your resolutions for the New Year, and a gold or yellow candle. Use sunflower oil and cinnamon oil to anoint the candle. Light the candle and reflect on what you want to accomplish and on what is standing in your way. Write out what you consider to be obstacles to your success. Then choose the top twelve obstacles and create a "List of Intent."

Each month, choose one obstacle from the list to deal with, starting with the most difficult and ending with the easiest. When you work with an obstacle, anoint a white candle with lemon oil and light. Imagine the issue overcome and eliminated. Write the issue on a piece of white paper and burn it. Repeat each month on a Sunday until you have worked with all the obstacles on your list.

Boudica

January 9
Monday

2nd ♋

Full Moon 2:30 am

☽ v/c 9:25 pm

☽ → ♌ 11:35 pm

Color of the day: Lavender
Incense of the day: Clary sage

Snowdrift Spell

With winter come the storms that cover the ground—and the roads—in a layer of fluffy white snow. When driving through the drifts, it's easy to get stuck. Here is a simple chant to help unlock the grip that the snowdrift has on your car. While rocking the car back and forth, either by using the gas pedal or with some friends pushing, repeat this verse:

> Snow that blows
> And snow that sifts,
> Loose my car
> From downy drifts.

Elizabeth Barrette

January 10
Tuesday

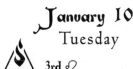 3rd ♌

Color of the day: Red
Incense of the day: Geranium

Fire Spell for Purging

Purging spells are a great way to clear away unwanted energy so you can start fresh. Fire is the perfect element for transforming a bad habit or pattern into a good one. Write whatever you wish to purge on a piece of paper. Fold the paper as small as you can while visualizing this unwanted presence in your life being crushed, growing smaller. Feel the power of courage within you that allows you to make whatever change you need in your life and turn negative to positive. Chant the following five times as you burn the paper safely in a heat-proof container:

> Transforming Fire,
> Bane to desire.

Allow the paper to burn completely and bury the ashes.

Ember Grant

January 11
Wednesday

 3rd ♌

Color of the day: Yellow
Incense of the day: Lavender

Deepen Awareness Meditation

Today is Woden's Day, which is ruled by Mercury. This is a good time to study, especially on things you've neglected. Are there any problems you haven't found solutions for? Is there anything you've wanted to gain further insight into but haven't found the time?

In sacrifice to himself, Woden (or Odin) hung on the Yggdrasil Tree for nine days and nights and discovered the hidden meanings of runes, the wisdom of the nine worlds, and magical songs.

Prepare an area you can devote to study. Chew some celery seeds, or drink peppermint tea. Read or meditate, and take notes for further study. Burn some lavender, clove, and lemongrass to assist in opening up your mind.

Maybe you'd like clarification on the meaning of a particular tarot card or rune. Write down your impressions. Burn a yellow or green candle anointed with oil of lime or clove. Expand your mind!

Kelly Proudfoot

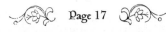

January 12
Thursday

3rd ♌

☽ v/c 3:23 am

☽ → ♍ 4:44 am

Color of the day: Green
Incense of the day: Jasmine

Spell for house Cleaning

With the Moon waning in Virgo, this is an excellent time to do house cleaning. If your tree is still up, maybe it's time to put away the ornaments and take down the tree. The holidays can be a stressful time, so banishing first is a good idea. Take a container of water, and stir in a pinch of salt, saying,

> *Element of Earth, cleanse and*
> *purify this water, so that it may*
> *cleanse and purify my house.*

Sprinkle water at the four directions in your home, or in the main room if you prefer, banishing any bad vibes that have accumulated. If you have a real tree, take it down, and send all the accumulated stress of the holidays into it. Burn it if possible, or take it to the curb and whisper thanks to the tree. Then, let all bad vibes go out with it.

Magenta

January 13
Friday

3rd ♍

☽ v/c 8:58 pm

Color of the day: Rose
Incense of the day: Alder

Midvintersblót

The ancient Norse people celebrated Midvintersblót on January 13. Offerings were made to Tiw (also called Tyr, Ziu, and Tiuz), a god of war and law-giving. From Tiw, we get the rune Tyr, which looks like an up-pointed arrow and symbolizes order, justice, and triumph. On this day, let's take a few minutes to think about the things that you consider worth fighting for, and then do a spell for justice. Draw the rune on a piece of paper, or pull it out of your rune set if you have one. Concentrate on the symbol for a minute, and then say the following:

> *Mighty Tyr, so strong and true*
> *Grant me justice that I am due*
> *Keep me strong so I might fight*
> *For all that's good, and kind,*
> *and right.*

Deborah Blake

 Page 18

January 14
Saturday

 3rd ♏

☽ → ♎ 8:28 am

Color of the day: Black
Incense of the day: Patchouli

Dream Interpretation Exercise

A great way to enhance your dream interpretations is to spend the day being hyper-observant of anything symbolic in your waking life. For example, if you're walking down a street and you see a barking dog, what does that represent to you? Is it a warning? We say a dog is "man's best friend," so could it represent a friend in trouble? Or a "yappy" aspect of yourself?

If the weather is prominent, is it stormy? Do you sometimes feel over-emotional?

Do you see a dilapidated house? Houses represent the mansion of the soul. Are you taking care of yourself?

What about food? Do you see delicious cakes filled with cream and dripping with chocolate that you either can't afford to buy or don't want to buy because of the calories? How often do you deny yourself pleasure?

Take notes and meditate on the meanings of anything you see.

Kelly Proudfoot

January 15
Sunday

3rd ♎

Color of the day: Yellow
Incense of the day: Eucalyptus

A hibernation Spell

We are deep in January, icicles hang from the eaves and my wood stove crackles as the flames dance. This would be a perfect day to "hibernate" and retreat for an hour—or a day. In winter, our homes become our dens, so why not enjoy them? Prepare a comfy spot for yourself. Surround your space with the things you love—a favorite movie, a cup of tea, or that book you haven't read yet. And invite a furry friend, if you share your home with one, to join you. Don't think of anything. Just be in the moment. If you wish, instead, slip into a deep meditative state. Linger. Let your spirit soar with the snow and ride the winter wind in your mind's eye. Return slowly to your normal state of mind. Sip your tea, open your book, and gaze out your window at the cold but beautiful whiteness of winter.

James Kambos

January 16
Monday

Martin Luther King, Jr. Day

 3rd ♎
4th Quarter 4:08 am
)) v/c 10:29 am
)) → ♏ 11:33 am

Color of the day: Silver
Incense of the day: Lily

I have a Dream Spell

Today marks the national celebration of the life and work of Dr. Martin Luther King. It's a time to remember how long and difficult the journey toward equality, freedom, and the dignity of all races and people has been. It's a time to honor the power of nonviolence, the ultimate practice of magic. Contemplate where you can bring more light into your life, look at where you could uplift your attitudes, behavior, thoughts, and beliefs.

Walk a simple spiral, circling in. With each step, identify what to let go of, or overcome, in order to uphold equality, freedom, and dignity for all. In the center, light a candle and chant:

Candle light, burning bright,
illuminate what is right,

Brighten darkness, lighten life,
overcome internal strife.

Spiral out. Know that magic changes energy, even internalized racism. Use this spell regularly to change old beliefs, and become free to pursue your dreams.

Dallas Jennifer Cobb

NOTES:

January 17
Tuesday

 4th ♏

Color of the day: Black
Incense of the day: Bayberry

Spell to Break Addictions and Bad habits

Addictions take many forms. A person can be addicted to a substance, to food, to sex, to gaming, to sleeping, and a number of other stimuli. What's more, a person can become addicted to certain patterns of thinking, such as paranoia, pessimism, or victim consciousness; or to emotions, such as anxiety, anger, or sadness. As magical practitioners, we must be extremely aware of these patterns, because dependencies of any type will hinder personal freedom.

To help break addictions, carry the herbs rue and yarrow, some sand, salt, and the stone amethyst on you in a small sachet bag. When you feel these addictive patterns rising up, bring your focus to the bag and "breathe" in its essence. Become aware of yourself, your body, and your mind.

Take the necessary steps both in the moment and in life to conquer any dependencies.

Raven Digitalis

January 18
Wednesday

🍎 4th ♏
☽ v/c 1:31 pm
☽ → ♐ 2:29 pm

Color of the day: Brown
Incense of the day: Lilac

Spell for health

Carnations are one of the flowers associated with the birth month of January. The carnation, while a standard florist's flower, is relatively inexpensive and comes in a rainbow of colors. The scent of the carnation is spicy and bracing. Carnations promote healing and healthy energy. This enchanting flower is associated with the element of Fire and the Sun. If you combine the energy of this fresh flower with the energy of the waning Moon today, you could banish illness and the blues right out of your life. Here is a little flower fascination to do just that.

> Carnations have a scent that's spicy and bold,
>
> They do banish sickness and troubles of old.
>
> May this flower fascination bring healing and peace,
>
> With the help of the waning Moon and the charm I speak.

Ellen Dugan

January 19
Thursday

 4th ♐

Color of the day: White
Incense of the day: Myrrh

Ritual for Sexual Healing

This day is dedicated to Caelestis, the Roman goddess of fertility, the Moon, and the heavens. Call on her to help you heal any challenging sexual issues stemming from abuse, negative body images, and so forth.

After sunset, bathe. Brew 2 cups of fenugreek tea and add a pinch of cinnamon. Sweeten tea to taste. Place a soy candle on your altar and light it as you say:

> *Caelestis, goddess of Earth and Sky, I call on you.*
>
> *Please heal me and bless me,*
>
> *Bring me into perfect harmony with the powerful life-force energy that is my sexuality so that I may shine.*

Place one cup of tea on the altar as an offering. Sit comfortably and gaze toward the altar as you drink the other cup of tea. As you share this moment with the Goddess, allow her to infuse you with her wisdom; her sparkly, healing light; and her divine sexual power.

Tess Whitehurst

January 20
Friday

4th ♐

☉ → ≈ 11:10 am
☽ v/c 4:49 pm
☽ → ♑ 5:40 pm

Color of the day: Pink
Incense of the day: Cypress

Refrigerator Love Spell

The bleak of winter can leave us depressed or lonely. It is hard to imagine warmth and love when it is cloudy, cold, and snowing. This is a love spell for yourself and your loved ones. The supplies are simple.

Find a photo of yourself and/or a loved one. If you don't have photos or a picture, make one, or use something that reminds you of the person. Place the picture in a refrigerator magnet frame or a recycled frame. Put it on your refrigerator. Write "You are Loved!" on a sticky note and put it on the photo of picture. Add a little rose oil to the frame, or a small plastic rose. You can cover your refrigerator with these little pictures and notes.

The framed photos will remind you and your loved ones that you and they are loved, and that there are many people in your life whom you love, as well. What could be more warming on a cold day?

Boudica

January 21
Saturday

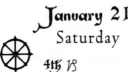

4th ♏

Color of the day: Blue
Incense of the day: Magnolia

hospitality and healing

This is a holy day in the Catholic Church honoring the martyrdom of Saint Meinrad of Einsiedeln. Clubbed to death by thieves wishing to steal pilgrims' offerings at the altar, Meinrad is remembered as the saint of hospitality. The church is also home to a beautiful Black Madonna, a miracle worker and healer.

As you begin your day, consider ways that you might offer shelter and hospitality to others, perhaps bringing needed healing and comfort to someone. Share a meal with a homeless person, pray in someone else's temple and leave offerings, or simply open to the miracles present in each moment and honor life as you live it. You might speak this prayer to the Divine Mother for her guidance as you seek to align yourself with the energies of openheartedness and service to others that this day inspires:

Black Goddess,

I witness so much suffering in the world,

Let me be a refuge to someone in need today.

Guide me as I open myself to the possibilities for healing I can offer and for love I can give.

Chandra Alexandre

NOTES:

January 22
Sunday

 4th ℣

☽ v/c 8:38 pm

☽ → ≈ 9:53 pm

Color of the day: Orange
Incense of the day: Frankincense

Express Freedom Charm

Have you felt hemmed in lately? If so, now is the time to embrace your freedom and dance in the Sun! The Sun enters Aquarius today—it's time to break free! Break the energy blockages that hold you back with this spell. Add the peels of one orange, rosemary, and sea salt to a warm bath. Charge the water with this charm:

Freedom is mine,
I proclaim to all,

Fill this water with cleansing power.

My future is sunny,
as I knock down the wall

I reclaim my purpose this month, day, and hour.

As you soak, feel the power of the Sun, creativity, and natural forces of the day combine with your spirit. You will emerge refreshed, and any energy blockages will be washed away. The future is wide open!

Mickie Mueller

January 23
Monday

Chinese New Year (dragon)

 4th ≈

New Moon 2:39 am

Color of the day: Gray
Incense of the day: Hyssop

Blossoming Spell
Recipe for New Beginnings

  8 ounces cauliflower florets

  6 ounces broccoli florets

  1 small carrot, sliced thin

  1 teaspoon cornstarch

  1 tablespoon water

  1 tablespoon cooking oil
    (canola, vegetable, or peanut)

  1 clove garlic, finely minced

  1 cup vegetable or chicken broth

  ½ teaspoon soy sauce

  1 egg white

1. Lightly steam the vegetables (crisp/tender) and set aside.
2. In a small bowl, add cornstarch to water, stir, and then set aside.
3. In large wok or fry pan, heat oil until hot, add garlic, fry for about 15 seconds (don't let it burn).
4. Add broth and soy sauce, and bring to a simmer.

5. Add cornstarch/ water to mixture, and simmer until it thickens.
6. Add egg white, gently swirling it through the sauce (don't beat it in).
7. Add steamed vegetables to heat through.

You may serve this as a side dish; or add chicken, crab, or shrimp to make a main dish.

Paniteowl

NOTES:

January 24
Tuesday

 1st ≈

Color of the day: Red
Incense of the day: Cedar

Compliment Day

Today is Compliment Day, and it was created in 1998 by Kathy Chamberlin and Debby Hoffman. Sincere compliments make people feel happy and valued. Celebrate this holiday by complimenting at least five people you meet during the day. This is a good opportunity to strengthen community ties in your coven or other magical group. You will need a piece of paper and a pen for each participant. The color pink symbolizes friendship, platonic love, and affection—so use pink paper or pink gel pens if possible. Each person should begin by writing their name at the top of the page. Then pass the papers deosil (clockwise) around the circle. Write down a nice compliment about the person as their page goes by. At the end, each person will have a collection of positive thoughts from everyone present. You may carry the page with you or keep it on your altar.

Elizabeth Barrette

January 25
Wednesday

 1st ≈

☽ v/c 3:33 am

☽ → ♓ 4:11 am

Color of the day: Topaz
Incense of the day: Honeysuckle

hot Toddy for a Cold or Flu

The winter months find us fending off invading hordes of cold and flu viruses. If you fall victim, brew up my medicine woman-grandmother's hot toddy for soothing relief. To make, put a thin "coin" of fresh, peeled ginger and healthy dollops of lemon juice and honey into a warm mug. Add a shot of bourbon or brandy, fill with boiling water, and sip while breathing the steam. The heat opens and relaxes airways and loosens phlegm, while ginger—a warming spice—relieves chills and stimulates energy movement through the chakras. Lemon juice kills germs and has antioxidant properties that help it fight infections and contribute to cell health and repair. Together, honey and lemon reduce fever and chills. Honey furnishes trace nutrients, has antibacterial and antiviral properties, and heightens feelings of well-being. The alcohol relaxes the body, quiets the mind, and induces sleep. Drink this before bedtime for a good night's rest and recovery.

Susan Pesznecker

History & Lore
January 25

If Saint Paul's day be faire and cleare,

It doth betide a happy yeare;

But if by chance it then should rain,

It will make deare all kinds of graine;

And if ye clouds make dark ye skie,

Then neats and fowles this year shall die;

If blustering winds do blow aloft,

Then wars shall trouble ye realm full oft.

Lee Obrien

January 26
Thursday

1st ♓
☽ v/c 11:53 pm

Color of the day: Green
Incense of the day: Clove

Solidify Your Financial Security

It's important to differentiate between what you want and what you actually need. When you have made the distinction, here's a spell that will assist in programming your environment and yourself to bring about financial security and growth. Anoint a green candle with basil oil and prepare a green mojo bag with an acorn, a nutmeg, a chestnut, a pinch of oak moss, and a piece of aventurine. Light the candle and hold the mojo bag in your left hand. Say aloud:

> I call on thee—Thor! Mighty protector of the common man! Please protect and enhance my financial well-being and block all obstacles to my success.

Imagine a golden orb pulsating over you and shooting out to zoom all over the world, attracting, like a magnet, all the opportunities that will assist you in maintaining and improving your financial status. Remember not to be greedy, or it will backfire. Carry the mojo bag with you.

Kelly Proudfoot

January 27
Friday

1st ♓
☽ → ♈ 1:28 pm

Color of the day: Coral
Incense of the day: Violet

Write a Memoir

Write a simple memoir about a psychic or magical experience. *Memoir* comes from the same root as *memory*, and is usually about a particular event or subject. Those "How I spent my summer vacation" essays we wrote in grade school are good examples of "simple" memoirs. This is not your autobiography, which would be a detailed account of your life. If you keep a journal, looking through it would be a good starting point. Think of an experience you have had that no one else has gone through, or that you have a unique perspective on. Write it as if you were writing a letter, or dictate it into a microphone, telling your story. Memoir is in the first person, and is more like writing fiction than reporting facts. How did you feel? Why do you remember this? What happened next? Put your thoughts in writing for yourself; if you like what you've written, show it to people when you are finished.

Magenta

January 28
Saturday

 1st ♈

Color of the day: Brown
Incense of the day: Pine

Clarity

Life can be hectic, and it is sometimes hard to keep our vision clear in the midst of the chaos of everyday life. Once the holidays are over and things have calmed down somewhat, take advantage of the winter's quiet to check in on your own mental clarity and make sure you are thinking as clearly as possible.

Place a bowl of water on your altar or any flat surface. Light a stick of incense—I like to use rosemary for this, since it is a herb that excels at sharpening the mind—or dab a few drops of rosemary essential oil on a white candle. Light the candle and place it where its light is reflected in the bowl of water. Watch the candle flicker and feel the air blowing away the cobwebs from your mind.

> *Powers of Air*
> *Gentle and fair*
> *Send me your light*
> *For clearness of sight*

Deborah Blake

January 29
Sunday

1st ♈

Color of the day: Yellow
Incense of the day: Marigold

Concordia: Birthday of Peace

The ancient birthday of the Roman goddess Pax (Peace), this day provides an opportunity to consider the benefits of removing ourselves from toxic situations so that peacefulness may be restored to us. It is also a wonderful day to take pause and rejoice in the harmony of our lives, even though we may know a thing or two about discord.

Whatever your situation, now is a good time to soak in the seas of calm and tranquility. Give yourself a moment of repose, making a bath of salts, gentle herbs such as lavender, and warm water. Soak, and let Pax flow on your every breath. You may wish to visualize her olive branch moving from the top of your head to the tip of your toes, removing any vestiges of upset, chaos, or anxiety. Release yourself into her arms saying, *In pace* (Latin for "in peace") over and over, first audibly and then in a whisper as you surrender even more deeply.

Chandra Alexandre

January 30
Monday

 1st ♈

☽ v/c 1:08 pm

☽ → ♉ 1:28 am

2nd Quarter 11:10 pm

Color of the day: White
Incense of the day: Neroli

Spell of Forgiveness

Before moving forward, sometimes we have to go back and mend our own "broken fences." Part of the mending is being able to forgive people for things we wish they hadn't said or done. It's not necessary to make a poppet, but you may if you have time. Alternatively, you can use a picture of the person, or simply write his or her name on a piece of cloth. Thread a large-eyed embroidery needle with a thick piece of string or yarn. Stitch around the edge of the cloth, pulling the yarn through tight enough to make a small pouch. Leave a few inches of yarn (long enough to use as a necklace or bracelet). Wear the pouch close to your skin for seven days. Think about what was said, or done, then consciously put it out of your mind.

On the seventh day, burn or bury the pouch, and again, consciously put the incident out of your mind, while saying three times:

I forgive this person.

This will allow you to not only forgive, but also forget about the hurt it caused you. Take back your power!

Paniteowl

NOTES:

January 31
Tuesday

2nd ♉

Color of the day: White
Incense of the day: Ylang-ylang

Resolution Renewal Spell

Today's the perfect day to renew your dedication to those resolutions you made at the beginning of the month.

Begin by revisiting your resolutions. Write them out again on a piece of paper. Now get honest. After a month, do they still seem doable and desirable? What roadblocks have you encountered? How can you shift your behavior or thoughts to really make them stick? Or perhaps you've had success and would like to add a few new ones. Based on your new insights, revise and/or revamp your list.

Fold the list three times, folding it toward yourself each time. Hold it between your two palms with your hands in prayer pose. Close your eyes, and visualize yourself triumphantly keeping your resolutions and living up to your highest ideals. Know in your heart that you can (and will!) it.

Finally, place the folded list on your altar and set a pyrite on top of it.

Tess Whitehurst

February

February is a month of extremes. It begins with the sabbat of Imbolc, has a romantic celebration of Valentines day mid-month, and just to keep us on our toes, February ends with an extra day some years. February is a magic in-between time where anything can happen. Often, the most brutal of winter storms occur now, and even though we get caught up in the romance of the middle of the month, and the revelry of Mardi Gras, spring can seem far away. But the light increases every day and we should remember that February is all about the light, possibilities, and the hope of new life to come. Deities associated with the month are the Celtic goddess Brigid and the Greek deities Eros and Aphrodite. Folks born in the month of February are assigned the violet and the primrose. The violet's magical qualities include faery magic and good luck and cheer, while the primrose has the enchanting qualities of protection and love. The amethyst is the birthstone for the month of February. A very popular stone with most magic users, the amethyst's magical properties include protection from manipulative magic and the power to enhance personal protection and your own spell casting.

Ellen Dugan

February 1
Wednesday

2nd ♉

 ☽ v/c 2:06 pm
☽ → ♊ 2:14 pm

Color of the day: White
Incense of the day: Marjoram

Freedom Spell

On this date in 1865, the 13th Amendment that outlawed slavery was signed by President Lincoln. In 1948, President Harry Truman signed the bill declaring today as National Freedom Day. Today, cast a spell for your own freedom. Ask yourself: What am I enslaved to? Where do I feel bound? What holds me back, or limits me? Write the answers down on a piece of paper. Over the sink or toilet bowl, burn the paper on a small plate. As the paper burns, affirm your freedom by saying:

> *No one owns me. I am free to*
> *be who I choose to be. I am free*
> *from fear and captivity. I am*
> *free to live peacefully.*

When the flame dies down, let the ashes cool. Pour them into your palm, gently rubbing both hands together, dissolving the ashes. Carefully, blow the last bits into the sink or toilet, and brush your hands together. Affirm by saying: *Done.*

Dallas Jennifer Cobb

February 2
Thursday

Imbolc
Groundhog Day

 2nd ♊

Color of the day: Turquoise
Incense of the day: Lily

A Divination Spell for Imbolc

Imbolc is a popular time for prophecy and divination. The land is beginning to stir from the depths of winter and everyone wonders how soon spring will come. Today, choose your preferred form of divination: tarot, scrying, runes, and so forth. If you don't practice divination regularly, or if you would like to try a new method, find a dark-colored bowl and add a few inches of water to the bowl. Set it on a table, and place a lighted candle to one side so the light reflects on the water. Gaze into the water, allowing your eyes to go out of focus and clear your mind, leaving it free for visions. As you prepare your divination technique, repeat this chant three times:

> *Seers of old,*
> *guide my sight,*
> *help me know*
> *dark and light.*
> *Help me find,*
> *let me see—*
> *as I will*
> *it shall be.*

Ember Grant

February 3
Friday

2nd ♊

Color of the day: Pink
Incense of the day: Rose

A Snow Angel Spell for Kids

The Earth may begin to stir with new life at this time of year, but some of the biggest snows still occur in February. And since kids are delighted by snow, take advantage of a snowy day to combine some fun activities for your kids with some protection magic as well. Bundle your children in warm clothes and go outside. Encourage them to make snow angels. Afterward, when they're occupied with other fun snow activities, you can create a little protection magic. Over the angel shapes they've made, say a silent blessing for each child. Next, sprinkle a small amount of a dried protective herb such as basil or rosemary on each angel. End your snow fun in the warmth of your kitchen over steaming cups of hot chocolate. No one has to know that you performed a bit of protection magic while having fun in the snow.

James Kambos

February 4
Saturday

2nd ♊
☽ v/c 12:06 am
☽ → ♋ 1:04 am

Color of the day: Black
Incense of the day: Patchouli

Banish Bad Vibes

Sometimes negative energy builds up. Now's a great time to clear those bad vibes out! Give your house a good top-to-bottom physical cleaning. Place a small pot in the center of the house, add one dried bean for every room, including closets. Now, starting at your front door, go room to room fanning sage or incense of your choice, making sure to get all the corners. "Lingering beasties, if you're against me, be you gone!" Then do the same ringing a bell. With a bowl of salt water, mark every window and door with a pentagram or equal-armed cross, saying, "By my word, this portal is sealed against all harm." Place the lid on the pot of beans, carry it outside, open the lid, and toss the beans far from your house. Rinse the pot with vinegar. Light a white candle in the center of your home.

Mickie Mueller

February 5
Sunday

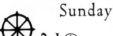 2nd ♋

Color of the day: Orange
Incense of the day: Hyacinth

Elemental Protection

In 1952, the country's first "Don't Walk" signs were installed in New York City. Our daily lives remain padded with mundane protection, but often we leave the house without magical support. Add magical insurance to your day with an elemental protection charm that invokes the strength, versatility, and security of the four guardians.

Use black ink to write the following on a strip of paper:

> As I wander through my day
> Many dangers come my way.
>
> Reaching deep and powers
> bring Guardians standing in
> a ring.

Roll up the paper strip, tie it with a red cord or yarn (for power), and carry it in a small bottle or mojo bag. Keep this talisman with you in a pocket, purse, briefcase, glove box, etc. Before heading out on an adventure, hold it in both hands and repeat the above charm as you imagine being surrounded by guardians of Earth, Air, Fire, and Water.

Susan Pesznecker

February 6
Monday

 2nd ♋
☽ v/c 7:31 am
☽ → ♌ 8:24 am

Color of the day: Ivory
Incense of the day: Rosemary

Aromatherapy to Reduce Stress in Your Home

Everyday stress and strain can be countered by performing a small cleanup of your home each evening that provides some aromatherapy. Use a mix of lavender and rose water to wipe down the bathroom sink in the evening. Bedrooms will benefit from the use of lavender buds in a dish or maybe some lavender oil in a small jar left open beside the bed. A bowl of potpourri made with rose and lavender will also provide some loving and calming essence in your living space. If you cannot use rose because of allergies, try jasmine, sandalwood, or cedar.

Boudica

February 7
Tuesday

 2nd ♌
Full Moon 4:54 pm

Color of the day: Maroon
Incense of the day: Ginger

Spell to Preserve the Moon

The Moon is full today, but if you are unable do a Full Moon ritual tonight, here's a spell to save Full Moon energy that you can do instead.

Gather several moonstones, white onyx, or other small white stones. Large beads work too, as long as they are minerals and not glass or plastic. You will need something to store the stones in; any container with a tight-fitting lid will work. Wash the stones in running water (no soap is necessary unless there is actual dirt on the stones). Before evening, decide which window in your home gets the most moonlight during the Full Moon; this will often be an east-facing window. Line the stones up on the windowsill covered with a white cloth, or place the stone, or stones, on a white cloth on a table. Hold your hands over the stones, and ask them to soak up lunar energy. The next morning, return them to the jar. When you need to use them, put them on your altar on the same white cloth.

Magenta

February 8
Wednesday

 3rd ♌
☽ v/c 11:42 am
☽ → ♍ 12:32 pm

Color of the day: Brown
Incense of the day: Lavender

Fight the Doubt Demons

In the depth of winter, the lack of light can lead to a darkness in our souls. Even the cheeriest person can start to be discouraged by the snow and the cold. Even warmer climates don't have the kind of energy during the winter that is around in the summer. The winter weather can drag us down and make us doubt ourselves.

Light a black or white candle and surround it with salt. Feel a circle of protective light surrounding you, full of the strength and comfort of the god or goddess you worship. Then say:

Demons of doubt
Who nip at my heels,
Who haunt my dreams,

Although you're not real
Get thee behind me.
Get thee away
From my circle of light.

You are banished this day.

Repeat as needed.

Deborah Blake

 Page 35

February 9
Thursday

 3rd ♍

Color of the day: Purple
Incense of the day: Myrrh

Fire Chant

Winter is the season for hearth fires. If you have a fireplace or a wood stove, you can build a fire and enjoy some of the oldest magic known to humankind. If you don't have a permanent hearth, you may wish to substitute with a smaller fire in a cauldron, or candleholders attached to a log.

The hearth is the heart of a home, and the fire is the light and warmth that gives power to the hearth. In ancient times, one of the home altars usually sat on or near the hearth, giving space to one of the many hearth goddesses. When you kindle a fire, say this chant to enhance its magic:

Fire of old, burn

Seasons of time, turn

Power of light, glow

Passion of love, flow

Elizabeth Barrette

February 10
Friday

 3rd ♍
☽ v/c 12:11 am
☽ → ♎ 2:54 pm

Color of the day: Rose
Incense of the day: Vanilla

An Awareness–Raising Meditation

To help facilitate spiritual awakening, contemplate the energy of items and people around you. What do they feel like? What do your senses and instincts tell you?

It is a good idea to keep a "manifestation journal" so you can observe how your thoughts, prayers, or spells influence what happens in your day-to-day reality. To help facilitate the awakening of your subtle senses, burn frankincense resin in your home on a regular basis while practicing deep breathing. During this meditation time, bring your focus to your five senses: sight, touch, taste, smell, and hearing. This small act of magic will help train your mind to go beyond the ordinary by utilizing the five physical senses and will, in turn, help to awaken your sixth sense.

Raven Digitalis

February 11
Saturday

3rd ♎

Color of the day: Blue
Incense of the day: Sage

Come Out of the Darkness

This is the day Bernadette Soubiroux saw the Virgin Mary in a grotto in Lourdes, which had also been a shrine to Persephone, goddess of the Underworld, who was taken there by Hades. Invoke Persephone today to assist you in overcoming darkness and coming back into the light.

Burn a black or indigo candle anointed with patchouli oil. Circle the candle with a ring of cypress, myrrh, and dittany of Crete. Hold a piece of jet in your right hand and meditate on your dark side and how the negativities came about.

See the darkness enter the piece of jet, and when done, throw the herbs, jet, and leftover herbs in a body of moving water, or bury in a hidden spot that won't be disturbed. Reward yourself by eating a pomegranate (Persephone's fruit) and contemplate your new lease on life.

Kelly Proudfoot

February 12
Sunday

3rd ♎

 ☽ v/c 4:09 pm
☽ → ♏ 5:01 pm

Color of the day: Gold
Incense of the day: Frankincense

Spell of Sunlight

Seasonal Affective Disorder (SAD) is understood to be a form of depression caused by the lack of sunlight during the winter. Although there are medications to combat SAD, we can also use meditation to overcome this seasonal disorder.

Each day, schedule 30 minutes for yourself. Find a comfortable place, and surround yourself with pillows. You can sit or lie down, whichever is more comfortable. Place candles around your area, and use mirrors to reflect the lights toward you. Play your favorite "summertime" music in the background—something that brings back memories of sunny days. Picture yourself lounging on a beach, playing baseball, or doing some other summertime activity you have enjoyed. Remember that the changing seasons on the Wheel of the Year promise things will change, and the dark times will be overcome by the light.

Paniteowl

February 13
Monday

 3rd ♏

Color of the day: Silver
Incense of the day: Clary sage

Parentalia

In ancient Rome, Parentalia, a festival to honor the deceased ancestors, was celebrated on February 13. Informal family dinners to honor the ancestral dead—considered helpful household spirits and known as "Lares"—were held.

Plan a family dinner and place an extra plate in the center of the table. Cover the plate with small white candles, bread, salt, and flowers. Before the meal, light the candles and invite your helpful ancestors with these words:

> *Our helpful ancestors we do embrace,*

> *In hopes that this gathering shall you grace,*

> *We honor you with blossoms, salt and bread,*

> *Bless this table and humble homestead.*

> *For all that you passed on to us we are grateful,*

> *May our kindest ancestral ties remain faithful.*

Leave the plate on the table until the candles burn out, then take the food and place it reverently outside as an offering.

Mickie Mueller

NOTES:

February 14
Tuesday

Valentine's Day

3rd ♏

☽ v/c 12:04 pm

4th Quarter 12:04 pm

☽ → ♐ 7:56 pm

Color of the day: Gray
Incense of the day: Cedar

A Rose Quartz Love Spell

This Valentine's Day spell combines the gentle vibration of rose quartz and the heat of ginger to draw love into your life. First, light a pink candle. Using a sheet of clean white paper, write down the qualities you're looking for in a romantic partner—without thinking of anyone specific. Then, sprinkle a pinch of ground ginger over the paper and place a piece of rose quartz on top. Wrap the paper around the rose quartz and tie up this bundle with a pink ribbon. Place the bundle on your altar, or in a secret place. If the ground isn't frozen you may bury the bundle, then unearth it when your wish has been answered. This spell may also be performed using a red candle, red ribbon, and cinnamon. However, the results may be unpredictable, and lead only to a brief affair.

James Kambos

February 15
Wednesday

4th ♐

Color of the day: Brown
Incense of the day: Sage

Lupercalia

In honor of the ancient Roman festival to purify the city, use this spell to purify your home.

Rosemary and sage are often used in purification and cleansing rituals. Mix dried rosemary and sage and place them inside a tea bag or wrap them in cheesecloth. Make an infusion by steeping the bag in near-boiling water, like making tea. Leave the bundle in the water until the water cools, then pour the liquid into a spray bottle. Use this water to mist the air in a room while chanting the following:

Purify and cleanse this place,
Clean and clear my living space.

Ember Grant

February 16
Thursday

 4th ♐
☽ v/c 11:03 pm

Color of the day: Green
Incense of the day: Carnation

health, Prosperity, and Wisdom

Today is National Almond Day so it's a good time to conduct a ritual to bring forth the energies for health, prosperity, and wisdom.

Consecrate a wand to Thoth (Egyptian scribe of the gods, who created hieroglyphs and is a god of healing). Make the wand out of almond-tree wood if you can, or anoint with almond oil.

Burn herbs such as amaranth, cinquefoil, and star anise, or make into potpourri, so you can enjoy it anytime you need a boost.

Anoint a blue candle with musk or nutmeg and inscribe it with your magical name or astrological symbol. Meditate on it as you see a blue orb of energy pulsate around you, enhancing your healing abilities for yourself and others.

Carry a piece of turquoise with you and eat almonds (they offer vitamin E and magnesium, and they build a healthy heart).

Kelly Proudfoot

February 17
Friday

 4th ♐
☽ → ♑ 12:03 am

Color of the day: White
Incense of the day: Orchid

Cultivate Grace

Friday is the traditional day of Venus, goddess of love, beauty, and fertility. Venus's energies include charm, composure, courtesy, and joy. In Latin, the noun *venus* is also linked to *venerari* (to honor or try to please) and *venia* (grace or favor).

Today, work powerful social magic, channeling Venus to create positive change. Consciously practice social grace and honor. When speaking to people, cultivate a deep sense of affection for them and express it through the tone of your voice. When listening, look deep into their eyes, and into their souls, really seeing and hearing them. Do not hold an agenda, but honor people by simply listening. Show them the courtesy of your undivided interest. Practice grace by acting, looking, and speaking in a gentle and kind manner, letting go of judgment. And because Friday is a day for relating and building relationships, your grace may invite Venus's blessings of love.

Dallas Jennifer Cobb

February 18
Saturday

4th ♑

Color of the day: Gray
Incense of the day: Ivy

Miracle healing Potion

This potion, like the Lourdes healing spring, can help cure what ails you.

Run a clean white quartz crystal under cold water for one minute. Place it in a wine glass or goblet. Add drinking water until the glass is almost full. Hold it in both hands and visualize it pulsating with very bright white light. Say:

Mother Mary, please infuse this water with vibrations of healing and love.

Cover the glass and set it near a picture of Mother Mary for one hour. Then, fill a tiny dropper bottle half with water from the glass and half with brandy. Pour the remainder of the water around the roots of a tree. For healing miracles, place 2 to 4 drops of the potion in your (or someone else's) drinking water or bath.

Tess Whitehurst

February 19
Sunday

4th ♑
☉ → ♓ 1:18 am
☽ v/c 4:22 am
☽ → ♒ 5:28 am

Color of the day: Orange
Incense of the day: Heliotrope

Protection Magic for Your Pets

If a strong bond is built between owners and their pet companions, their energies are open to each other in perfect love and perfect trust. Because animals have fewer inhibitions and judgments than their human companions, their spirits are naturally open and receptive to subtle forces. When making prayers or spells designed to influence your pet (such as to give them healing, protection, or longevity), you should burn a corresponding elemental candle. If your pet is terrestrial, burn a brown candle; if water-bound, burn blue; if winged, burn yellow; and if amphibian, burn red. While burning the candle, focus on its light and pray to any spirits, deities, or forces you wish. When the candle has burned down, put the stub and any associated spell or prayer items in a drawstring bag and hang it up in your home.

Raven Digitalis

February 20
Monday
Presidents' Day
(observed)

4th ♒

Color of the day: Lavender
Incense of the day: Lily

Chocolate Magic

Winter is the time for chocolate magic. Chocolate's antioxidants stimulate endorphins and brim with passion and power, while also echoing feminine magics. The earthy, spicy heat is quite remarkable, and the resulting brew makes a nice backdrop for elemental protection spells.

Use individually wrapped flat squares of chocolate as a magical canvas. Open one edge, remove the chocolate, and with a toothpick, inscribe words, symbols, or runes on the square. Return the chocolate to its wrapper, charge or bless, and it's ready for use. Add other magical correspondences to focus the energy. Dark-chocolate orange squares with orange oil added speak of solar energies, joy, and warmth. Chocolate-mint squares boost mental clarity, while chocolate-raspberry supports feminine magic and love spells. Eat the chocolate or melt into coffee.

Susan Pesznecker

February 21
Tuesday

Mardi Gras (Fat Tuesday)

 4th ≈
γ v/c 11:17 am
☽ → ♓ 12:31 pm
New Moon 5:35 pm

Color of the day: Red
Incense of the day: Ylang-ylang

New Moon Magic

There is a New Moon today, and it's Mardi Gras! This is a perfect day to tap into the celebratory vibe and welcome new beginnings and opportunities. You can use a taper candle or a votive candle in a votive cup. Use whichever style you prefer. Light a purple, gold, and green candle, not only for Mardi Gras but for a touch of color magic. The color purple enhances power, green encourages prosperity, and gold is for success. If you like, you could add some Mardi Gras beads, coins, and other accessories to your altar set up. Take a few moments and meditate on this New Moon and all the possibilities it brings, and link into that energy. Then light the candles and repeat the spell verse.

*Purple for power,
now come to me,*

*While the green promotes
prosperity,*

*The gold is for riches,
fame and success,*

*May my New Moon magic truly
be blessed.*

*Let the good times roll,
is what they say.*

The magic begins this very day.

Allow the candles to burn in a safe place until they go out on their own.

Ellen Dugan

Notes:

February 22
Wednesday

Ash Wednesday

 1st ♏

☽ v/c 9:24 pm

Color of the day: Yellow
Incense of the day: Lilac

Reversing Spell

Sometimes we feel we are working under some kind of restriction. We may feel covered by a cloud, or a curse, or some kind of spell working. Be it a jealous friend, some stupid troll, or we just got in the line of fire, we are looking at the feeling that we have been hexed. A reversing or uncrossing can help remove the issue. A bath of rose, lavender, Bay laurel, and lemon oil will open the door for the individual to cross from under the working. This is followed by a ritual of meditation to find the root cause and banish the curse. Then, residual bad energies are cleared away and replaced with healing energy. Finally, a ring of protection against further attack is created. The hardest step is finding the root cause. You must be honest with yourself. Who or what is the cause? Examine closely what caused the issue.

Boudica

February 23
Thursday

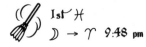 1st ♏

☽ → ♈ 9:48 pm

Color of the day: Purple
Incense of the day: Balsam

Terminalia: A Day of Endings

The last day of the ancient Roman year is called Terminalia, and it was celebrated on this day. We officially celebrate endings, doing so on three levels: gross, subtle, and causal.

First, take care of the physical. You may wish to remove things from a desk, pantry, or closet that are past their usefulness.

Next, take care of your psychic and emotional space. Wrap yarn or a thread between your pinky and thumb of the same hand to symbolize the lingering connections you have to past loves, friends, or foes. Sever these ties one at a time by cutting each thread after you honor the lessons of the relationship.

Now is also the time to bring an appropriate end to magic work completed or left in process. Take care of leftover ritual items and altars. Return things to their proper place today; finish, or let go of, what you started, and get ready to begin anew.

As you tie up all loose ends, visualize and then firmly establish your boundaries with the concretizing Sanskrit syllables: HUM PHAT.

Chandra Alexandre

NOTES:

February 24
Friday

1st ♈

Color of the day: White
Incense of the day: Cypress

Meltwater Spell

Water is an element of transformation. It constantly shifts from cloud to rain, river to vapor, trickle to ice. It carries the energy of change in all its forms. By harnessing the power of water, you can work to manifest desired changes in your life.

For this spell you need a clean, resealable glass bottle and some glitter. Go outside on a cold, sunny day and find some icicles. Hold the bottle underneath an icicle to catch the meltwater as it drips. Then say:

> Water clear and bright
>
> Changing, taking flight
>
> Go from cold to warm
>
> Help me to transform.

Add a few pinches of glitter, then seal the bottle. Whenever you need to change something, shake the bottle and watch it swirl. Remember the energy of the icicles changing to water. Focus that energy on your goal.

Elizabeth Barrette

February 25
Saturday

1st ♈

Color of the day: Indigo
Incense of the day: Rue

Snowdrop Spell

The snowdrop is a garden flower associated with the winter months, and also with our last sabbat, Imbolc. Another name for the snowdrop is Candlemas Bells. Its astrological correspondence is the planet Saturn. I have always assigned the element of Earth to this little beauty. In the language of flowers, the snowdrop promises consolation, and it brings hope during the coldest and bleakest time of the year. Since Saturday is linked to Saturn's energy, let's work a little flower fascination with the energies of the waxing Moon and bring about some change and optimism today.

> The snowdrop blossoms during the darkest, coldest days,
>
> But it brings hope and consolation in many ways.
>
> I call for positive change and new opportunities,
>
> I put the past behind, and look forward to what will be.

Ellen Dugan

February 26
Sunday

1st ♈
☽ v/c 7:52 am

☽ → ♉ 9:29 am

Color of the day: Amber
Incense of the day: Juniper

Forgiveness

They say that to err is human but to forgive is divine. But you don't need to be a god or goddess to forgive those who have wronged you. Just remember that we are all human, and flawed, and that most folks are doing the best they can.

Light a white candle and some lavender incense (or dab a bit of lavender essential oil on the candle—lavender is good for both love and peace, so is perfect for this spell). Say:

> To err is human
>
> To forgive is divine
>
> Grant me forgiveness
>
> In heart and mind

Deborah Blake

February 27
Monday

 1st ♉

Color of the day: Gray
Incense of the day: Hyssop

hair Growth Tonic

To encourage healthy, thick hair, and/or to help your hair grow faster, use this simple tonic.

Bring a pot of water to a boil. Add a handful of dried nettles. Reduce heat, cover, and simmer for 10 minutes. During this time, chant the following three times, consciously directing the energy and intention of the chant into the pot:

Thick like the neck of a bull,
Strong like the trunk of an oak,

Bright like sunlight on water,
Full like the bounty of the Earth.

More gloriously than a king (or queen), I am crowned.

Remove the pot from the heat and allow liquid to cool. Remove nettles. Place cooled liquid in a spray bottle and add 4 to 7 drops of rosemary essential oil. Spray freshly washed hair with the growth tonic (shake well before using) and gently massage with your fingertips. Continue until your desired look is achieved, replenishing your supply as necessary.

Tess Whitehurst

February 28
Tuesday

 1st ♉

☽ v/c 2:46 pm

☽ → ♊ 10:27 pm

Color of the day: Black
Incense of the day: Basil

Spell for Wisdom

Sometimes, we all wish we knew "what's going on" in our professional or personal lives. We get anxious and often overreact in situations. We'd like a mentor in our lives who could guide us in making good, sound decisions. What we often overlook is the fact that we DO have examples in our lives who seem to be able to navigate stormy times with grace and aplomb.

A simple spell to invoke the wisdom you have seen in others is to picture that person sitting across from you and handing you a scroll that gives a "recipe" for strength, courage, and understanding. This is when those old photos of ancestors come in quite handy for focusing on attributes that come with your bloodlines. Using the image of that person, simply say:

Please show me the wisdom
you've learned through the
years ... Help me to face my
challenge and fears.

Paniteowl

February 29
Wednesday
Leap Day

 1st ♊
2nd Quarter 8:21 pm

Color of the day: Topaz
Incense of the day: Honeysuckle

Charm for Laundry

Leap Day is, according to Roman traditions, good for doing spells for improbable purposes. So here is a charm for laundry. Do you have problems with lost socks? Underwear isn't there, or your pants have a great big hole when they come out of the dryer? Here's a charm to protect your clothes and keep them from straying. Take a holey sock, and fill it with dryer lint and a few pennies found on the street. Hang this over the washer and dryer and chant:

Save my clothes, save my socks,

Save the trousers, and the

frocks, Keep my pants and my

caps safe from falling through

the gaps.

Recite the charm before you wash your clothes, and don't overfill the washer. If you use a laundromat, keep the sock with you in your laundry basket or bag, and mutter the charm to yourself before you put in your laundry.

Magenta

NOTES:

March

M arch is a time of the year when anything can and does happen. Some days are warm. You can soak up the Sun, and feel the promises of the summer stirring in your heart. Other days, an icy wind can chill you and have you clutching a jacket close. It's enchanting to watch daffodils and crocuses push their way up, proving that once again, life has reclaimed the Earth. It's an exciting time of change, heralding in the Vernal Equinox. Trees have begun to produce small, smooth buds on their bare branches, and nature is really pushing those buds to swell and pop forth with blossoms of all kinds, showering the world with color. I always think of March as nature's last snooze under the warm blankets in the morning, and now she must rise and face the shining day! It's a month all about breaking inertia, new beginnings, and potential. Magically, this is the perfect time to begin a new project and to take advantage of all the new growth energy in the air. It's also a perfect time to cast a spell to clear out what no longer serves us. Use the March winds to blow away the old, dead leaves and reveal new life.

Mickie Mueller

March 1
Thursday

 2nd ♊

Color of the day: Turquoise
Incense of the day: Balsam

Find and Enhance Sexual Love Spell

Profane love is just as important as divine love. It can be hard for people without a partner to feel the heat of the season. If you're looking for a mate, try this ritual—using two candles and two glasses of wine. Just leave the second glass and candle on the windowsill for your lover to find you.

Make covet powder as follows: Grind together cardamom, caraway, coriander, chili pepper, and clove. Sprinkle a pinch into two glasses of warmed wine. Burn red rose and dragonsblood. Anoint two red candles with oil of cinnamon, consecrated to Bast. Play flute music in the background. Whether single or not, sip the wine and meditate on the candle. As you do, visualize Bast circling you and intoxicating you with her sensuous energies. The rest is up to you!

Kelly Proudfoot

March 2
Friday

 2nd ♊
☽ v/c 8:14 am
☽ → ♋ 10:08 am

Color of the day: Rose
Incense of the day: Thyme

Wishing Well
(Feast Day of St. Claud)

In ancient times, the waters of many wells were considered sacred, said to bestow wisdom, bring healing, and generate luck for those who drank from them. People made pilgrimages to these sites, leaving offerings as thank-you tokens for the gifts and blessings received. Today, create your own wishing well and invite others to the party! Start with a pot, cauldron, or chalice filled with water and spend some minutes singing, chanting, or intoning your intention:

Waters pure and clear, you are the gateway to eternity;

A wishing well that we might drink in the wisdom of the ages;

A wishing well that we might heal the wounds of old;

A wishing well that we might open to your magic.

Let everyone take a turn at the well, and after a time of contemplation or prayer and a small sip of water, invite them to leave a dime to honor the spirit of the well. Silver affirms the water's power and the number 10 helps to actualize the wish.

Chandra Alexandre

NOTES:

March 3
Saturday

2nd ♋

Color of the day: Blue
Incense of the day: Sage

A Poppet Spell for Spring

Poppets and dolls have been used in magic since ancient times. And, since today is the Doll Festival in Japan, this spell is appropriate for today. Poppets were once used in spells to encourage spring to return. To do this, make a poppet using any green fabric. Before sewing the poppet closed, fill it with plant materials associated with growth and fertility. Apple seeds, nuts, oak twigs, grasses, and pine needles are some good choices.

Whatever materials you use, make sure you use three different varieties. After you've closed the poppet, use a fabric marker to enhance it with symbols of abundance and good fortune. These could include a Sun or star shape, male and female symbols, or a simple sketch depicting a sheaf or grain. When finished, release the poppet into a stream or river. Breathe deeply and visualize the world becoming green again.

James Kambos

March 4
Sunday

 2nd ♋
☽ v/c 5:17 pm
☽ → ♌ 6:17 pm

Color of the day: Yellow
Incense of the day: Almond

Daffodil Spell

The jaunty and sunny daffodil is a symbol of spring. It is associated with the planet Venus and the element of Water. In the language of flowers, the daffodil symbolizes chivalry, which can be an important thing in our modern world. Honestly, can't we all use a touch of good manners and gallantry in our lives? As we have a waxing Moon today, let's work a little magic to pull this type of energy into our lives. See what happens when you purposefully give out kindness to another.

> March has just begun, and the
> spring is not far away,
>
> I call for magic and chivalry to
> come my way,
>
> I will receive as well as return
> this gallant request,
>
> Returning compliments and
> generosity with zest.

Ellen Dugan

March 5
Monday

2nd ♌

Color of the day: Lavender
Incense of the day: Neroli

Flower Blessing

With spring come the flowers. They burst up from the ground after a long winter's sleep. Their colors brighten a world of browns and grays. They bring positive energy and hidden messages. Honor them with this blessing:

> Bless the snowdrops,
> Nodding and white.
>
> Bless the crocus,
> Purple and bright.
>
> Bless the jonquils,
> Trumpets of gold.
>
> Bless the tulips,
> Painted so bold.
>
> Bless the flowers,
> Heralds of spring;
>
> Crown the Goddess
> Of everything.

Elizabeth Barrette

March 6
Tuesday

2nd ♌

☽ v/c 8:27 pm

☽ → ♍ 10:27 pm

Color of the day: Scarlet
Incense of the day: Ylang-ylang

Take Action

Mars's energy of adventure, competition, action, and strength rules on Tuesday. Take action today toward what you want to become, and set into motion your plans and dreams. Enjoy longer, faster walks outside as the days lengthen. While you walk, feel the strength of your body, heart, and lungs. Breathe deeply and be inspired to pursue what you want, and with each step know that you move ever closer. What seeds do you want to plant within? Chant as you walk:

> With each step,
> I plant the seeds,
>
> With each breath,
> my passion freed,
>
> With each moment,
> I cultivate change,
>
> My life in joy I rearrange.

As you walk, you will notice an energy shift, and you will feel uplifted, inspired, and ready to pursue your dreams.

Dallas Jennifer Cobb

March 7
Wednesday

2nd ♍

Color of the day: Yellow
Incense of the day: Bay laurel

Overcome Shyness

As the first bulbs peek their heads up out of the ground in celebration of the coming of spring, use this energy for growth and overcoming shyness. Put a tulip or some other spring flower on your altar when it is still closed. Say the spell and feel yourself opening up as the flower does!

> Strength for courage
> Make me bold.
>
> Help me blossom
> Out of the cold.
>
> Make me brave
> And help me shine.
>
> Social graces
> Now are mine.

Deborah Blake

March 8
Thursday

2nd ♏

☽ v/c 4:39 am

🌕 Full Moon 4:39 am

☽ → ♎ 11:50 pm

Color of the day: Green
Incense of the day: Nutmeg

Full Moon Spell

Use this is the last Full Moon of winter (in the Northern Hemisphere) to contemplate endings and beginnings. Let's be mindful of the Wheel and the promise of the Goddess—the cycle of life, death, and rebirth. Have we slept through the long, cold time of death, and are we ready for the time of rebirth? Did we take inventory of our successes and failures in the past year? Have we resolved issues that blocked our successes? Are we ready to shed our outer layers, like snakes shed their skins, for the time of new growth?

As we look at the Moon, the ever-present reminder of the Goddess, we ask her to help us shed our old troubles and worries and leave the baggage of last season/year behind—hopefully resolved. We still have time before the season of renewal to resolve old challenges and think about moving to new tasks and new challenges. This Moon asks: "Are you ready?"

Boudica

March 9
Friday

3rd ♎

Color of the day: Pink
Incense of the day: Alder

Inner and Outer Beauty Ritual

Breathtaking beauty is never just skin deep; it's the result of an interconnected balance between inner and outer allure. This ritual is great for anytime you'd like to enhance your appearance and appeal.

The yin/yang symbol is a partnership of polarities; it helps us establish the holistic balance that characterizes exquisite and timeless beauty.

Draw the symbol and place it beneath a white votive candle on a small dish. Surround it with a few simple representations of beauty, such as blossoms, petals, or crystals. Light the candle and sit comfortably before it. When you feel centered, say:

> In all ways,
> I am balanced.
>
> In all ways,
> I am serene.
>
> Inside and out,
> I am beauty incarnate,
>
> I calmly shine my light
> into the world.

Continue to relax as you imagine the yin/yang entering your third eye and filling your entire body and aura with its energy.

Tess Whitehurst

NOTES:

March 10
Saturday

3rd ♎

☽ v/c 10:09 pm

Color of the day: Black
Incense of the day: Magnolia

Time-Management Spell

We hear people say it every day: There just isn't enough time, or, there aren't enough hours in the day. We could all use awareness of how we use our time. Use this spell to enchant a watch, clock, or other timepiece so you can better organize your time-management skills and be aware of using your time wisely. Saturday is named for the Roman god Saturn—we know him as Father Time. This is a good day to work on making the best use of the time you have—either at work or in your personal life. Place the timepiece on a table or your altar; burn dark blue, black, or brown candles; and chant the following:

Time is precious,
night and day,

Help me use it, work or play.

Make the most of every minute,

With this spell I now begin it.

Ember Grant

March 11
Sunday

Daylight Saving Time begins, 2 am

 3rd ♎

☽ → ♏ 12:24 am

Color of the day: Amber
Incense of the day: Thyme

here Comes the Sun!

If you have a warm day today, create a Sun-filled infusion to soothe your heart and fill you with happiness. Heat a coffee mug of water and mix in 3 tablespoons of honey. Fill a large jar (about a one-gallon size) with cool water, including the honey water. Add 3 round slices of lemon. Drop in 4 bags of Roobios tea, also known as redbush tea or bush tea. Put the lid on the jar and set the jar where sunshine will hit it most of the day. Bless it by saying:

> Darling sunshine,
> I welcome you,
>
> Fill this vessel with your
> warming rays.
>
> As I create this magical brew,
> Please fill it with your
> shining ways.

The golden brew will fill you with well-being for your mind, body, and spirit.

Mickie Mueller

March 12
Monday

3rd ♏

☽ v/c 2:30 pm

Color of the day: White
Incense of the day: Rosemary

Enchant Your Morning Coffee

If you're anything like me, caffeine is one of your first thoughts upon awakening. For most people, caffeine is not a harmful addiction. (At the same time, for those who are addicted, I recommend occasionally cutting caffeine out of your diet as a sort of "caffeine fast," to ensure that your body isn't overly dependent!) To add an extra bit of buzz, stir your coffee (or tea!) and focus on the liquid's beautiful pattern. Put down the spoon and smell the brew. After a deep inhalation, say:

> This elixir is enchanted,
> this brew is pure.
>
> This blend is filled with aware-
> ness, motivation, inspiration,
> joy, and psychic sight.
>
> So mote it be.

To add extra potency, try bringing your mouth close to the drink and intoning or chanting words with which you'd like to enchant your beverage, such as "love," "peace," or "inspiration."

Raven Digitalis

March 13
Tuesday

3rd ♏

☽ → ♐ 2:54 am

Color of the day: Gray
Incense of the day: Bayberry

Honoring Women

The great philosopher Socrates was taught by Diotima, a woman who was "wise in love and many other kinds of knowledge." While perhaps overshadowed by her pupil through the writings of history, it is her shoulders upon which much of Western philosophy stands. Today then is a day to reflect upon the impact of those women who have taught you, served as your helper, provided you with guidance, and supported you in your endeavors of the mind, heart, and soul. If there is someone among them who is most special to you, then perhaps it's time to write a letter describing the ways in which this woman has touched your life. If she is alive, have the courage to mail or read the letter to her aloud. If she has crossed over, read the letter as an offering to the cosmos so she hears.

Chandra Alexandre

March 14
Wednesday

3rd ♐

4th Quarter 9:25 pm

Color of the day: Topaz
Incense of the day: Marjoram

Spell of Inner Knowledge

Before doing a spell, it's often wise to remember the warning, "The first thing a spell changes is you!" A spell is a commitment to effect change. Are you willing to accept the consequences? Are you constantly trying to change something in your life without committing yourself to working on you? Maybe it's time for you to do some mirror magic! Sit in front of a three-sided mirror. Notice the different ways you see yourself, looking first at the middle mirror, then at both side mirrors. Now, smile and observe. Now, frown and observe. Now, make an angry face and observe. Now, make a poker face and observe. Which face is most natural for you? Which face would you most like people to remember? Choose the face that most reflects the way you see the world. Cast a spell to achieve the wearing of the face that will most make you happy. It's as simple as saying, "This is me, this is who I want to be." Then simply do it!

Paniteowl

March 15
Thursday

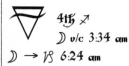

4th ♐
☽ v/c 3:34 am

☽ → ♑ 6:24 am

Color of the day: Crimson
Incense of the day: Apricot

Cauldron Blessing

Historically a day dedicated to Mediterranean Earth Mother goddesses such as Rhea and Cybele, it's a perfect time to bring out your brewing pots. Whether for kitchen or magical work of other varieties, pots are the containers of our conjuring in the material realm, the symbolic wombs we tend and care for in order to birth our creations. To bless these tools, take them outdoors and put them on the Earth, upside down. Create a paste of water and soil, adding a drop of your own blood if you wish to consecrate the mixture. Then, coat the outside of the pot. Place stones, flowers, and other Earth-honoring objects on top, much like decorating a cake. Once the coating is dry, offer the following:

> Crucible, container,
>
> cauldron, pot—
>
> serve me well,
>
> the Earth you're not;

> But into my house
>
> now blessed we go—
>
> the power of Earth
>
> this does bestow.

Dust off the pot, cleaning it if you wish with water (or not). Bury the ornaments or place them under a tree as offerings.

Chandra Alexandre

NOTES:

March 16
Friday

4th ♍

Color of the day: Coral
Incense of the day: Thyme

A Spell for Abundance

At this time of year, sap begins to rise in every tree and plant. The sap is rich with minerals; it is the essence of the Life Force. From the most majestic oak tree to a humble blade of grass, sap vitalizes the entire plant kingdom! Here is a spell that utilizes this seasonal energy to bring abundance. If possible, cut a few stems of some early blooming shrubs or trees such as forsythia, quince, or cherry. Place them in a vase of water upon your altar. On either side light a green candle and in front set a dish of soil. Feel the soil, crumble it in your fingers, and inhale its earthy scent. When you feel connected to this Earth energy speak these words:

> Now the green season begins,
> And all nature stirs again.

> I ask that the Divine Spirit
> bless me with abundance,
> wealth, and prosperity.

Leave the stems upon your altar for a few days.

James Kambos

March 17
Saturday
St. Patrick's Day

4th ♍
☽ v/c 9:00 am

☽ → ♒ 12:11 pm

Color of the day: Blue
Incense of the day: Patchouli

A Spell to Banish Negative Energy or Emotions

You'll need a tall black taper candle, olive oil, matches, a stone, an abalone shell (or other thurible), and a candle snuffer.

Anoint the candle with oil, working from top to bottom, As you work, speak aloud about what you wish to banish, thus sealing your intentions into the candle. Set the stone in the shell and hold the candle aloft at an angle, allowing the wax to drip onto the stone as you continue speaking about that which you wish to banish. Invoke the words *noli me tangere* ("Let nothing touch/harm me") as the wax carries the banished concerns to the Earth (stone) to hold. When finished, snuff the candle and place it and the stone on your altar for a least a Moon cycle.

For best results, work this spell at the New Moon. Using metamorphic rock—granite or marble—is ideal, as it withstands tremendous force and only becomes stronger.

Susan Pesznecker

March 18
Sunday

 4th ≈

Color of the day: Gold
Incense of the day: Eucalyptus

Anti-Fire Spell

Make up four packets as follows. Take a square sheet of white paper, between 5 and 8 inches on a side. Draw the alchemical symbol for Fire, a triangle pointing up, in red ink, and allow it to dry. On top of it, draw the alchemical symbol for Water, a triangle point down, in blue ink. Put a generous pinch of salt on this. Fold the corners into the center, chanting:

> *Safe from harm,*
>
> *Safe and warm,*
>
> *Fire glow but do not burn.*

Then, fold the corners in to the center again, and finally a third time. Tilt the packet so the salt is at one side. Seal the center securely with several drops of blue candle wax; use the same candle for all four packets. Put the packets in the corners of your house or apartment, preferably someplace inconspicuous. This spell should be renewed every few years, or anytime you move.

Magenta

March 19
Monday

 4th ≈
☽ v/c 4:31 pm
☽ → ♓ 8:05 pm

Color of the day: Ivory
Incense of the day: Narcissus

Escape with the Swallow to a Sacred Space

Contemplate the return of the Swallows to Capistrano on this day before the Spring Equinox. If you don't already have a sacred space to retreat to, create one! Carry a piece of silver and of moonstone today, and meditate on your escape to your peaceful place. Allow the swallow to guide you. Combine poplar, sandalwood, and mugwort for a sacred incense to use in your cauldron. Build a swallow's nest out of mud and straw, and then place it on your altar. Anoint a silver or white candle with myrrh, and ask the swallow to show you a path to peace. Escape into your sacred space. Read the tarot, or conduct any divination that feels right to you. Meditate on the candle and see the swallows returning to Capistrano. Hear them call. Feel their influence speaking to your sense of security and your feelings of spirituality and protection.

Kelly Proudfoot

March 20
Tuesday
Ostara – Spring Equinox

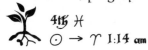

4th ♓

☉ → ♈ 1:14 am

Color of the day: White
Incense of the day: Geranium

Sweet Creation

Honor the sacred union of Maiden Goddess and young Sun God that results in conception. Plant seeds inside you that will grow with the growing light. Choose ancient symbols of fertility, sacred union, and conception—candy eggs or jelly beans—in green, yellow, and purple to represent fertile Earth, the growing Sun, and the sacred union.

Know what you seed. Choose three goals—one physical, one mental, and one spiritual. Charge the green egg, with your physical goal, and say:

> I plant the seeds of physical health and fitness.

Eat it. Then, imbue the yellow egg, with your mental goal, and say:

> I plant the seeds of mindfulness.

Eat it. Finally, empower the purple egg with your spiritual goal, and say:

> I plant the seeds of the divine in my soul.

Eat the sweet. Now, sip some water, face the Sun, and say:

> I water and feed my intentions,
>
> May they grow strong like the Sun God
>
> And full like the Goddess.
>
> So Mote It Be.

Dallas Jennifer Cobb

Notes:

March 21
Wednesday

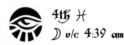

4th ♓
☽ v/c 4:39 am

Color of the day: Brown
Incense of the day: Honeysuckle

Dark of the Moon Spell with hecate

Today is the dark of the Moon. The Moon will not be seen at all in the sky, This is the time of dark magic and mystery, and a perfect time to call on Hecate, the patron of witches and sorcerers, to see what lessons she may have for us. Her symbols are keys, cauldrons, and the crossroads. Don't be surprised if you notice howling dogs when you call upon Hecate. They sense when she is near. Tonight, as darkness falls, light a purple candle and call on the goddess of the Crossroads and meditate on her. Here is a little invocation to get the magic rolling. Blessed be!

> Hecate, triple-faced Maiden, Mother, and Crone,
>
> I honor your presence in my life, hearth, and home.
>
> During this dark of the Moon, I call you near,
>
> I sit, eager to learn and ready to hear.

March 22
Thursday

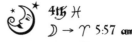

4th ♓
☽ → ♈ 5:57 am

New Moon 10:37 am

Color of the day: White
Incense of the day: Mulberry

See in the Dark Spell

The absence of the Moon in the night sky symbolizes nothingness and emptiness. Because the Moon is just about to wax, personal energies will begin to increase for the next two weeks. Luna represents the internal, the emotional, and the psychic. This is the time for new beginnings. Lie flat on your back under the moonless sky for at least twenty minutes. Bring your focus to the stars (if the night is clear) and contemplate the true meaning of infinity: a fact of nature that is literally impossible for us humans to fully comprehend. While looking at the stars, say the following, or something similar:

> Moonless sky, endless cosmos,
>
> I come before you as a pure child of the Universe.
>
> Open my mind to your limitlessness,

Ellen Dugan

Reveal the unseen, and forever illuminate my perception.

So mote it be.

The waxing Moon will help increase these spiritual energies in you, especially if you perform this ritual nightly until the Full Moon. Note any spiritual awakenings or consciousness-alterations you experience throughout.

Raven Digitalis

NOTES:

March 23
Friday

1st ♈

Color of the day: Purple
Incense of the day: Rose

Tubilustrium Festival

This is the last day of the Mars festival, when war-trumpets and weapons were cleansed. A small remembrance of those who serve would be appropriate today. It's time to remove the roadblocks to peace.

Meditate today and remember those who have fought so bravely for our freedoms. No matter what their sex or culture, they have put their lives on the line for us. Remember our peacekeepers, those who work for our safety each day. They too are warriors and deserve our special attention.

Finally, do a meditation for peace. Ask yourself what it is you can do to bring peace into the world. From asking for divine intervention to creating peace in your home, see if you can bring just a little bit of the intention and energy of peace to your small corner of the world.

Boudica

March 24
Saturday

1st ♈

☽ v/c 1:17 pm

☽ → ♉ 5:43 pm

Color of the day: Brown
Incense of the day: Sandalwood

Creativity

As we start to move into spring, it is nice to take a day or two before things get more hectic to focus on our creativity. If you have one particular area in which you prefer to be creative—writing, painting, sewing—allow yourself a day to "play" in a creative way. Maybe have some friends over for a beading party or fingerpaint with the kids. Anything that helps you tap into your inner child and let your creativity loose. To prepare, say this spell over whatever tools you will be using:

Spark of inspiration

Joy of mind and heart

Help me be creative

As I craft my art

Deborah Blake

March 25
Sunday

1st ♉

Color of the day: Orange
Incense of the day: Marigold

Pecan Day

Today is Pecan Day. The pecan tree, a native to North America, grows up to 100 feet tall and may live over 400 years. A single tree can produce several hundred pounds of nuts. The tree and its nuts attract many species of wildlife.

The Algonquin Indians gave us the name "pecan" from the original term *paccan*, for a nut that must be cracked with a stone. In Texas, the Mariame tribe revered the pecan tree as sacred, much as some European tribes honored the oak or the ash. It represented the Great Spirit to them. The nuts formed a major part of their diet.

If pecan trees can grow in your area, consider planting one. Otherwise, celebrate this holiday by eating pecans. They are popular used in ice cream, candy, and pies. You can also find recipes for making spiced, candied pecans.

Elizabeth Barrette

March 26
Monday

 1st ♉

Color of the day: Gray
Incense of the day: Rosemary

An Unusual Love Spell

Too often, when someone says, "love spell" we think of either "sex" or "life mate." But there are many kinds of love, such as love of one's parents and siblings, love of the Divine, or love for friends.

If you wish to, cast a spell to increase the amount of affection and friendship in your life. Get several candles and candle holders. One should be your favorite color. The other candles should be a variety of colors you like and consider attractive. Put the favorite-color candle in the center of your altar and light it. Surround it with the other candles, and light them, one by one, naming them with traits you want in your friends. These could be humor, compassion, strength, honesty, and so on. Move these candles closer and closer to your own, and feel yourself attracting people with these qualities into your life.

Magenta

March 27
Tuesday

 1st ♉

☽ v/c 12:35 am

☽ → ♊ 6:43 am

Color of the day: Red
Incense of the day: Cinnamon

Spell for Birthing

Whether it is child birthing, or creating a work of art, or even writing an article or a book, there is pain in creation. Physical, emotional, and spiritual stress come into play when we are bringing a new life into the world. This birthing spell calls on the element of Fire to help us deal with great effort necessary to achieve something wonderful. You'll need:

> 1 cup of potting soil
>
> 1 cup of spring water
>
> a pinch of salt
>
> a pinch of cinnamon
>
> a white votive candles
>
> a small pan
>
> a small bowl
>
> a wooden spoon

1. Place the soil, water, salt, and cinnamon in the pan and bring it to a boil on your stove. Use a wooden spoon to stir in a widdershins motion as the mixture begins to

bubble. This keeps the mixture from overcooking. (To stir it UP, you'd be using a deosil motion.) As you stir, chant softly:

> Water, Earth, Fire, and Air,
> give to me a thing most fair.

2. Take the pan from the stove and pour the mixture into the bowl. Place the bowl on a table.
3. Light the three candles. Allow the candles to burn completely.
4. Take the cooled mixture and sprinkle it outside your door, or if necessary, put it in a small flower pot.

As you go into "labor," think of the prepared soil and the spell that you created to control the pain or anxiety as you stirred the pot.

Paniteowl

NOTES:

 Page 66

March 28
Wednesday

1st ♊

Color of the day: Yellow
Incense of the day: Bay laurel

Ace this Project Spell

Creative energy is all around you during the spring; here's a spell to bless a new project. You'll need an orange candle, a cinnamon stick, and a deck of tarot cards. You'll be using all four aces to bring balance to your project. Arrange the cards around the candle, light the candle, and, holding the cinnamon stick in your hand, meditate a bit on the tarot images before you. Letting the light from the orange candle warm you, rub the cinnamon stick between your hands to warm it, and smell the scent. Repeat the following:

> I have an ace within my heart,
>
> And now this project
> will make a start,
>
> Bringing creative energy
>
> A great success this
> now shall be!

Leave the cinnamon stick next to the candle, and let the candle burn out. The cinnamon stick should be kept with you and will be your talisman for this project.

Mickey Mueller

March 29
Thursday

1st ♊
☽ v/c 2:05 pm
☽ → ♋ 7:07 pm

Color of the day: Green
Incense of the day: Jasmine

Hand-Wash Money Spell

Make an infusion of dried basil leaves by wrapping them in cheesecloth and steeping like tea in boiling water. Allow the basil-infused water to cool, then pour it into a basin or bowl. Wash your hands with this water as you visualize prosperity as needed in your life. Chant the following:

> Basil bring prosperity—
>
> Wealth, abundance,
>
> Grant to me.
>
> Help me in my time of need,
>
> With harm to none so mote
> it me.

You may store this basil rinse for several days and repeat the washing until you have used all the water. Dispose of the herbs in your yard or compost bin.

Ember Grant

March 30
Friday

 1st ♋
2nd Quarter 3:41 pm

Color of the day: White
Incense of the day: Mint

Egg Magic

Eggs are potent symbols of fertility and reference the ongoing, interconnected cycles of life and birth. Bless each egg before using, and offer thanks as the egg is cracked.

Cook with eggs: Make a quiche, custard pie, or deviled eggs. Serve an all-the-eggs-you-can-eat breakfast! Meditate on the circular forms as symbols of solar energies.

Dye eggs with natural colors. Simmer eggs with onion skins for golden-brown eggs, or in pureed beets for pink, or parsley for green. Use a white crayon to inscribe a symbol or rune on the shell before dying: perhaps Fehu (new journeys), Ihwaz (transformation), or a simple cosmic spiral. Or dye eggs with concentrated vegetable food colors: green for prosperity, blue for peace, red for energy, yellow for success, purple for the mysteries.

Rinse the used eggshells and crumble them over your planting beds. They will add calcium to the soil as well as solar and fertility influences.

Susan Pesznecker

March 31
Saturday

 2nd ♋

Color of the day: Gray
Incense of the day: Rue

Lighthouse Ritual to Find Your Way

Do you feel buffeted by life like a lost ship at sea? This lighthouse ritual can help you find your direction and guide you to solid ground.

Obtain a small figurine or picture of a lighthouse. Immerse it in dry sea salt for ten minutes and then charge it in sunlight for one minute. After dark, place it on your altar near a white tea light candle, light it, and say:

> Lighthouse, lighthouse light
> my night
>
> Connect me with my
> truest sight
>
> Soothe my darkness
> with your glow
>
> So that my right path
> I shall know.

Allow the candle to burn all the way down. Tomorrow night, replace the tea light with another one. Light it, repeat the chant, and allow it to burn all the way down. Repeat once more the following night.

Tess Whitehurst

April

There is so much going on in the month of April! There is April Fool's Day, and it's National Poetry Month. It's also the anniversary of the sinking of the Titanic and the opening of the first McDonalds. We celebrate the birthdays of Hans Christian Andersen, Leonardo da Vinci, Sherlock Holmes, and Daffy Duck. But what is April really all about? What is it that makes April special? April marks the real end of winter. Daffodils pop open and nod their yellow heads. Grass starts to recover from its frozen cover of snow, trees bud, forsythia shows its yellow cloak, tulips display their lips, and the small animals—chipmunks, squirrels, rabbits and other animals—wake up from their winter sleep. The promise of renewal is realized as the sun removes the icy chill from the air. Rain soaks the earth, prompting growth and preparing the flowers of the season. And we find ourselves shedding our winter coats on the first warm spring day. This is April!

Boudica

April 1
Sunday
April Fools' Day – Palm Sunday

 2nd ♋
)) v/c 12:20 am
)) → ♌ 4:35 am

Color of the day: Gold
Incense of the day: Eucalyptus

Rama Navani

Today is Rama Navani, a Hindu festival celebrating the birth of Rama, an incarnation of Vishnu. People celebrate it with recitals, chanting, and music, and by lighting lamps at shrines and temples. In some places, parades carry images of Rama through the streets.

Rama is known as the lord of self-control, or lord of virtue. He represents adherence to right behavior even in the face of adversity. As a ruler, he governs with peace, prosperity, and justice. These qualities attract his followers, such as Hanuman the Monkey King. For people in leadership roles, Rama offers guidance in meeting duty with courage and compassion. For others, he represents devotion and loyalty. Reading about his adventures is a good way to explore self-discipline and fulfillment. This god can also help break bad habits or anything else that stands in the way of meeting your responsibilities.

Elizabeth Barrette

April 2
Monday

 2nd ♌

Color of the day: Silver
Incense of the day: Lily

Celebrate the Child within You

To honor Hans Christian Andersen's birthday and International Children's Book Day, read to children or to yourself—maybe choose a book that you loved as a child. Or write a children's story! Help out at your local library, or create a poster to inspire the love of reading. Include your own artwork and a message to children. Dedicate this day to all mythological creatures in the world of children's literature, and make an offering of milk and honey to the fairies of your garden. (Even read aloud to them!) Burn incense made of jasmine, sandalwood, lavender, and valerian. Or scatter around your offering of milk and honey. Carry a piece of rose quartz or turquoise in a pink or lavender mojo bag, along with a piece of angelica that has been anointed with jasmine oil. Sniff it every now and then, and allow your mind to drift back to happy memories of childhood.

Kelly Proudfoot

April 3
Tuesday

2nd ♌

☽ v/c 9:47 am
☽ → ♍ 9:53 am

Color of the day: White
Incense of the day: Bayberry

Daisy Spell

The daisy is a symbol for cheer and innocence, and wearing a fresh daisy is thought to promote love. Working with the energy of the waxing Moon, let's conjure up a flower fascination with the daisy.

> *A symbol of cheer and a pert little flower,*
>
> *Daisy, now lend to me your magical power.*
>
> *Bring happiness and love into my life,*
>
> *This quick little charm, will work out just right.*
>
> *A merry Garden Witch's spell has now been spun,*
>
> *As I will so mote it be, and let it harm none.*

Allow the flower to work its magic until it begins to fade. Then return it to nature.

Ellen Dugan

April 4
Wednesday

2nd ♍

Color of the day: White
Incense of the day: Lilac

Activate Your Ability to heal

You are a healer, and you are called to activate your healing abilities and to share your gifts with the world.

Brew a cup of peppermint tea. Sit comfortably in a relaxing atmosphere, perhaps before your altar. Silently declare your intention to embrace your destiny as a healer. Then, hold the cup in both hands, close your eyes, and visualize bright rainbow-colored light coming down from above, entering the crown of your head, going down to your heart, and out through your hands into the cup. Feel it swirling with this light. Then, mindfully, drink the tea.

When you're finished, close your eyes and request a visit from a guide, deity, or totem that would like to help, and simply be open to any thoughts or visions you receive. Even if you think nothing is happening, know that you are receiving exactly the guidance you seek on a subconscious level.

Tess Whitehurst

April 5
Thursday

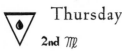

2nd ♏

☽ v/c 1:37 am

☽ → ♎ 11:32 am

Color of the day: Crimson
Incense of the day: Clove

Water Spell

April showers bring May flowers. Save your glass bottles from spaghetti sauce, pickles, fruits, and so forth bring to gather rain water for all types of spell work! .

Wash the bottles well, including the lids. Set them outside to gather rainwater all through this month. Cap the full bottles and place them in a cool, dark space. Before using the rain water, place some of the jars outside and leave them overnight during the Full Moon. Do the same with the remaining jars during the New Moon to achieve the most effective results. Be sure to mark each jar so you will know by which Moon it was charged.

Paniteowl

April 6
Friday

Good Friday

2nd ♎

Full Moon 3:19 pm

Color of the day: Coral
Incense of the day: Vanilla

Awaken Goodness

Today is Good Friday in the Christian faith, and also a Full Moon that is known by many names. The April Full Moon was called Seed Moon in Medieval England, Planter's Moon in Colonial America, and Peony Moon in China. The Celts called it Growing Moon, and Neo-pagans know it as Awakening Moon. Combining these popular meanings, cast a spell for "awakening goodness" with the full energy of the Moon. Take a sheet of paper, and quickly write the numbers one through ten on the left side. Just as quickly, write down ten good things in your life. These can be people, places, things, thoughts, or practices. The trick is to not hesitate or think, simply free-associate and write down what you comes to your mind. By writing these down you have successfully worked awakening magic. By moving energy from within yourself to create positive change, you have shifted your focus to the good.

Manifest goodness on the physical plane and make it real, by taking action. Choose one person, place, thing, thought, or practice from your list, and take time to visit, call, practice, or honor it (or them). We awaken goodness all around us by consciously practicing gratitude for what is good in life.

Dallas Jennifer Cobb

NOTES:

April 7
Saturday

Passover begins
3rd ♎
☽ v/c 6:15 am
☽ → ♏ 11:18 am

Color of the day: Black
Incense of the day: Ivy

Job Spell

While you search the newspapers looking for that perfect job, here is some help to get that interview! Cut out the job that you are qualified for and place the ad under a pentacle on a sacred space, sprinkle with thyme, and add a magnet. Ask your higher power for the chance to interview. Concentrate on your will, making this manifest, and say:

> I want this job,
> I need this job,
> I am qualified for this job.

Call for the interview, or send the requested résumé and cover letter. If you need help polishing it up, ask someone to help you. All you need, you will receive. And be sure you follow up the call and résumé. Be persistent. Every day, return to the ad and ask again for the chance to interview. Ten days is time enough for a response. If you receive no response, the job was not meant for you.

Boudica

April 8
Sunday
Easter

3rd ♏

Color of the day: Amber
Incense of the day: Heliotrope

Get Creative with Crystals

Quartz crystals are a very common and valuable tool in the witch's bag of tricks. Quartz crystals are said to amplify the energy of anything they are "attuned" to. While I'm not big on New Age lingo myself, many of the New Age movement's concepts have validity and are rooted in ancient esoteric spirituality. Where crystals and gemstones are concerned, numerous people from various cultures and walks of life utilize the Earth's healing and transformative properties directly from the minerals. The next time you perform a spell, add a boost of power to the working at hand. Add the quartz crystal to the various spell components, whether it's a sachet bag, charm, candle spell with herbs, a tea, potion, bath brew, or anything else that uses physical ingredients. When you weave your magic, meditate on the intention by putting the quartz to your third eye, and add it to the spell to multiply your power!

Raven Digitalis

April 9
Monday

3rd ♏
☽ v/c 2:56 am
☽ → ♐ 11:12 am

Color of the day: Ivory
Incense of the day: Hyssop

Cultivate Creative Passion

Do your creative energies need a boost? Whether it's for writing a novel, finding a mate, communicating with a coworker more effectively, or finishing that cable-knit sweater you started years ago, today is the day to open to your creative drive and turn on the juice for life. Begin by putting some fire back into your soul's expression in the world with the following affirmation:

> I am Divine and glorious.
> A whole universe of possibilities
> lies within me.

Bring your spirit out to play. Dress up. Wear red. Kiss yourself in the mirror. Invite a stranger to lunch. Send yourself a sultry poem. Sing out loud on the bus. Whatever you do, honor the unique spark of the Divine that you are. As an extra token of your willingness to live courageously and desire to invite in creative passion, anoint your brow with peppermint and your heart with cinnamon oil.

Chandra Alexandre

April 10
Tuesday

3rd ♐

Color of the day: Cedar
Incense of the day: Maroon

Bicycle Blessing

If you ride a bicycle for pleasure or exercise, try this bicycle blessing. Take a bowl of water, a little salt and a stick of incense. Stand next to the bike, face east, and cast a circle. Take the water, and say:

> Blessings on you,
> element of Water.

Then, take a pinch of salt, toss it in the water, and say:

> Blessings on you, element of
> Earth, that together you will
> purify the world.

Walk around the bike clockwise, sprinkling the water, and say:

> Goddess, protect this bicycle,
> may it always be safe, and carry
> me swiftly where I wish to go.
> So Mote It Be!

Then light the incense, walk around the bike and say:

> Goddess, protect this bicycle,
> may it always be visible
> to other vehicles, and invisible
> to thieves. So Mote It Be.

Then close the circle.

Magenta

April 11
Wednesday

3rd ♐
☽ v/c 7:06 am
☽ → ♑ 1:02 pm

Color of the day: Brown
Incense of the day: Marjoram

Oracle at Praeneste Day

The Oracle at Praeneste, which belonged to the goddess Fortuna, was a very popular shrine in Italy. On April 11, people would travel to the shrine to have their questions answered by drawing oak slips from a jar. You can have fun with this tradition by doing a little divination of your own. On slips of paper write four "yes" responses and four "no" responses. On the back of each, draw a wheel with eight spokes—Fortuna's symbol. Fold the papers, drop them in a decorative jar or bowl, and mix them. Light some frankincense incense and a white candle. Then, petition Fortuna with these words:

> Lady Fortuna smile upon me,
>
> I ask you sincerely these
> questions three.

Ask three questions, one at a time, and draw an answer for each question.

Mickie Mueller

April 12
Thursday

 3rd ♑

Color of the day: Purple
Incense of the day: Myrrh

Celebrate the Grain Goddess

In ancient Rome, today marked the beginning of the Cerealia, a week-long celebration honoring Ceres, the grain goddess. She was held in high regard by farmers and is believed to have shared her knowledge of agriculture with mortals. Begin this day by making your breakfast a ritual, and let your kitchen table become an altar. Prepare and eat your cereal mindfully; savor the aroma of your toast. If it's possible, have your family eat breakfast together, and visualize fields of grain ripening. It's easy to forget in our modern high-tech world that the domestication of humble grains, such as wheat and corn, fueled the beginning of civilization. If you perform any rituals today, focus on fertility and growth. Place a dish of grain or cereal on your altar as a centerpiece. And today, cover your altar with a simple white cloth and burn only white candles. White is the color that represents Ceres.

Raven Digitalis

April 13
Friday

Orthodox Good Friday

 3rd ♑
4th Quarter 6:50 am
☽ v/c 1:05 pm

☽ → ♒ 5:48 pm

Color of the day: Pink
Incense of the day: Orchid

Good Luck Spell

Some people think Friday the 13th is bad luck. There is a general belief that both Fridays and the number 13 are unlucky. And some unlucky things have happened on this day: the Knights Templar were all arrested on a Friday the 13th in 1307. However, witches believe that what may be bad luck for others symbolizes good luck to us—like black cats, for instance! And Pagans know that covens often have thirteen members, and Fridays are Freya's night—the perfect night for ritual. So gather thirteen of your friends and have a party, or celebrate today with thirteen good things to eat. Witches make their own luck, so feel free to say this short spell.

Friday the 13th,
just another day.

I feel lucky,
let's keep it that way!

Deborah Blake

April 14
Saturday

Passover ends

4th ≈

Color of the day: Indigo
Incense of the day: Pine

A Spell for Change

Find a stone that you don't mind parting with and focus on it, using it to symbolize a bad habit that you'd like to change. Hold the stone and visualize your goal filling it. Chant the following:

> Water flows, carves the land;
>
> Change occurs at its hand.
>
> Make a change in my life;
>
> Whatever's wrong, set it right.
>
> For good of all and harm to none.
>
> As I will, so it be done.

Bury the stone and pour water over the soil. The elements of Water and Earth are both ruled by Saturn—put this change in his hands.

Ember Grant

April 15
Sunday

Orthodox Easter

 4th ♒
☽ v/c 6:42 pm

Color of the day: Gold
Incense of the day: Eucalyptus

Ritual for Winged Feet and Blessed Sneakers

Bless your walking shoes with this simple ritual. Gather a pen, small bit of paper, matches, salt, water, candle, and thurible. Write this charm on the paper:

> Strong my heart,
> And fleet my feet,
> Soon to start,
> My blood to beat.
>
> Send me power
> That I may last
> For minutes and hours
> Along this path.

Dissolve a bit of salt in the water. Light the candle. Pass the shoes above the candle and say:

> By Fire and Air
> I bless these shoes.

Dip your fingers into the salt water and sprinkle it over the shoes and say:

> By Earth and Water
> I bless these shoes.

Read the charm aloud, then place the paper in the thurible and light it. Visualize the charm's power being concentrated by the flame. Dip a finger into the cooled ashes and draw the rune Uruz—for strength and vitality—inside each shoe. See the aura of empowerment glowing around your sneakers!

Susan Pesznecker

NOTES:

April 16
Monday

 4th ♒
🌙 → ♓ 1:38 am

Color of the day: Silver
Incense of the day: Clary sage

happy home Spell

Monday, the Moon's day, is connected to emotions, home, and happiness. It is a good day to clean and organize and to cast a Happy Home Spell to cleanse and protect your home with happiness and love. Using dried sage or sweet grass, smudge your house, moving from the front door, clockwise throughout the space. In every room, envision the smoke gathering negativity, and the negativity evaporating along with the smoke. Stop by windows and doorways and say:

> Home and portals now be clear,
> happiness and love abides here.

Return to the front door and carefully smudge the entrance and say:

> Bless those who enter here,
> Let them be loving, happy,
> and clear.

Draw a pentagram, inviting elemental protection, and say:

> Earth, Air, Fire Water,
> protect the children,
> mothers, and fathers.

> Unto all let it be known this is
> a safe and happy home.

Dallas Jennifer Cobb

NOTES:

April 17
Tuesday

 4th ♓
☽ v/c 10:34 am

Color of the day: Red
Incense of the day: Geranium

Frost Spell

Early in spring, sap rises. The flowers begin to bloom. Trees and bushes open their buds to reveal fresh green leaves. The first warm breezes bring the world back to life as the Sun heats the dark earth. Yet winter is not quite out of reach. A single cold snap can sheathe the world in ice, killing the tender young plants.

When a frost alert comes, start by covering plants with a frost cloth or layer of mulch wherever possible. Then say this chant over plants you wish to protect:

Sun's ray and fire's glow,

Shield tender blooms and leaves

*From frost and winds
that blow—*

This blanket magic weaves.

Visualize the sunlight condensing into a layer of golden cloth that drapes over your plants. Remove it the next morning after the danger of frost has passed.

Elizabeth Barrette

April 18
Wednesday

 4th ♓
☽ → ♈ 11:59 am

Color of the day: Yellow
Incense of the day: Lilac

Break a Love Spell with Lilies

Lilies have the power to break love spells, so if you tried one and it went sour, or you feel you are under the influence of another person's magic, here is a spell to break those ties. Gather fresh lilies from the garden or the florist and tap into the powers of the waning Moon to help diminish the original magic.

*This flower fascination has a
simple task,*

*Break that old love spell, and
call the energy back.*

*May these fresh lilies be a
symbol for me,*

*Hearts are no longer bound
and our wills are free.*

*As the flowers fade, so too does
that silly old spell,*

*Any harmful effects are gone,
and all will be well.*

Allow the lilies to stay in your home in their vase until they begin to fade naturally. Then add them to your yard waste to be recycled.

Ellen Dugan

NOTES:

History & Lore of the Lily

A tablet found in Sumeria, and believed to be about 5,000 years old, tells about a city that was surrounded by lilies. Historians believe that lilies spread from Persia on caravans of nomads, who ate the edible root bulbs.

The ancient Greeks held lilies in very high esteem and associated the plant and its flower with Hera. The Romans adopted the Greek respect for the Madonna lily and associated it with their gods. Soldiers carried the roots with them for food, and they used it to make a salve that could be used on wounds and burns.

Lee Obrien

April 19
Thursday

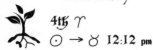

4th ♈

☉ → ♉ 12:12 pm

Color of the day: Green
Incense of the day: Carnation

Spell for New Beginnings

Meditation helps us visualize what we want to achieve, but the most valuable spell is the one that teaches us about the actual process of new beginnings. Patience is the key word here.

Fill a clay flower pot with a good potting soil. Choose seeds that have a special meaning to you. It doesn't matter whether you use herb, or flower, or even a vegetable seed, the point is to prepare a place for a seed to grow. Plant the seeds, water them well, and place them somewhere they will receive warmth. Yes, the ideal would be in direct sunlight, but you can also put the pot on top of your refrigerator. Have you ever noticed what a warm surface that is? Water the seeds gently each day and watch for the sprouts to start.

At some point, you will probably have to "thin" the planting. I know that is hard to do, but this process teaches us that in order for a healthy plant to survive, we must be able to remove some shoots. We should also realize that as we undertake a new project, or a new job, or a new home, or a new partnership, there will be things we'll have to "cut out" in order for our new beginning to flourish and bear fruit. This is a simple lesson-in-life spell you can do anytime to remind yourself of what can become real if you simply nourish and protect your efforts.

Paniteowl

NOTES:

April 20
Friday

 4th ♈
☽ v/c 3:35 pm

Color of the day: Pink
Incense of the day: Violet

herald the Prophesy

Awaken the soothsayer in you by undertaking a light fast, perhaps foregoing your afternoon coffee and snack or eating only fruits throughout the day. Limiting food intake, even to a small degree, is a time-tested way to induce altered states of consciousness. Today is a good day to offer your concentration to the subtle realm where indications of what's to come are waiting to be let into awareness. At the start of the day, offer a prayer to ask the beings of that world to communicate with you through sign and synchronicity. Then, pay attention! Take in the omens. At the end of the day, use magazine images to form a collage. Let your intuitive response guide you to create a montage of impressions. Like the Oracle of Delphi, your prophesy will be revealed through contemplation on the riddle of your assembled pictures.

Chandra Alexandre

April 21
Saturday

 4th ♈
☽ → ♉ 12:05 am

New Moon 3:18 am

Color of the day: Gray
Incense of the day: Sage

familiar Blessing

In ancient Rome, April 21st was Parilia Day, in honor of Pales, a pastoral deity. Traditionally, on this day animals were driven through purifying fires. Later, it became a day for Christians to take animals to church for the Catholic Blessing of the Animals. Today, give thanks for the animals in your life, and most especially for those that act as your magical familiars. Stand or sit in front of your altar with your animal, or put a picture of the "darlin' beastie" on your altar if he or she won't sit still. Light a brown candle (or one in the shape of your animal) and say:

> I give thanks for the blessing of this animal companion, friend, and familiar
>
> May the gods bless (him/her) in return
>
> And keep (him/her) safe from all harm
>
> So mote it be

Deborah Blake

April 22
Sunday
Earth Day

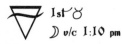

1st ♉
☽ v/c 1:10 pm

Color of the day: Orange
Incense of the day: Almond

Let's Keep Our Planet Green

On this Earth Day let's get out and plant to keep our planet green. And since this Earth Day falls on a Sunday, we'll also be able to tap into some solar energy. Go out today and plant just one plant. This could be a tree, a perennial, an herb, a houseplant, or a packet of seeds. Visualize the garden tool you're using, whether it's a shovel, hoe, or trowel, as your magic wand. Let your garden tool connect you with the Earth's energy, until you feel your hand tingling. In the bottom of your planting hole place one penny as a token of thanks to Mother Earth. Planting one plant today may seem like such a small gesture, but just think what a huge impact it would have on our planet if we all did that today. Nurture your plant, and as it grows feel your connection with the Earth deepen.

James Kambos

April 23
Monday

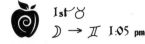

1st ♉
☽ → ♊ 1:05 pm

Color of the day: Lavender
Incense of the day: Neroli

Healing for Beginners

The power of touch has amazing curative properties in the hands of a healer. But it also has amazing abilities in the hands of a loved one. When a child is sick, nothing helps them get better faster than some loving touch showing that you care.

You don't need to be a trained Reiki person to be able to send healing energies to your child. Sitting the child on your lap, holding them, placing your hands on their head and heart will start a process of love and energy that even the child will recognize is helping them. They may ask what you are doing, and feel free to tell them you are giving them love and healing energy to help them get over their sickness, or help them through their sickness. Touch is a powerful tool. It shows you care, and it tells child they are loved.

Boudica

April 24
Tuesday

1st ♊

Color of the day: Black
Incense of the day: Ginger

St. Mark's Dream Weaver Ritual

Historically, unmarried women in Britain would perform a ritual on this day to dream of their future mate. This tradition-inspired ritual will induce you to make contact—via your dreams—with your truest love in this lifetime. This won't be "just" a dream, but an actual date, albeit on the astral plane. Unlike the St. Mark customs of yore, you need not be single to perform this ritual. After all, even happy couples can benefit from a bit of dream-time romance (though there is no guarantee about who, exactly, you will see).

After nightfall, invoke St. Mark's assistance. Bake a cake without vocalizing a single noise the entire time. Silently empower the batter with your intention to connect with your beloved in the astral plane. While it's cooling, get ready for bed. At midnight, eat a piece of cake. Then, immediately approach your bed, get into it backwards, and call it a night.

Tess Whitehurst

April 25
Wednesday

1st ♊
☽ v/c 4:31 pm

Color of the day: Topaz
Incense of the day: Lavender

Robigalia

The Romans celebrated an agricultural festival this time of year, to ensure a good growing season. A successful harvest begins with the planting. Literally, or metaphorically, plant some seeds today that you hope to harvest later this year. This can include making plans for something you want to achieve or the planning or planting of an actual garden. Speak this chant as you plant or prepare your goals:

Some things I want

Some things I need

To reach my goal

I plant this seed.

Ember Grant

April 26
Thursday

 1st ♊
☽ → ♋ 1:42 am

Color of the day: Jasmine
Incense of the day: White

Cosmic Invocation by Starlight

This is a fun magical working to perform by starlight on any clear-skied evening. Simply go outside and breathe in the essence of the night. Feel the presence of mystical darkness surrounding you; contemplate the endlessness of the cosmos and the immaculacy of the natural world around you. When you feel grounded and centered, bring your focus to a star, raise your hands, and draw its essence into a point of your body. Repeat this for different points on your body, using different stars for each point. (My suggestions include working on the chakra points, the joints, wrists, elbows, knees, hands, feet, and so on.) This working will help connect you with the cosmos and the mysteries of life. For extra potency, spend some time beforehand researching astronomy and astrology, and the physical and metaphysical universe. You may also wish to wear glitter when performing this working. Doing so can help you connect the stars above with the sparkles on your body—as above, so below.

Raven Digitalis

April 27
Friday

 1st ♋

Color of the day: Purple
Incense of the day: Yarrow

Your Dream Vacation

You'd like to travel around the world, or maybe just to Paris. But the budget doesn't allow for any farther than the next town. You'd like to climb mountains, but you have two toddlers to care for. What can you do? The key to having an interesting life is preparing so that life can work in mysterious ways. "If you want your ship to come in, you must build a dock." Work on building your docks. Gather materials—a cruise catalog, information from the tourist bureau, whatever will help you visualize. If you want to travel where another language is spoken, learn that language. Put yourself in a relaxed state, and visualize yourself in the specific place you wish to go—at the top of the Eiffel Tower, or on the beach in Cancun. Affirm that you will visit that place, and spend a few minutes every day doing this visualization.

Magenta

April 28
Saturday

1st ♋

☽ v/c 3:05 am

☽ → ♌ 12:10 pm

Color of the day: Blue
Incense of the day: Magnolia

Floralia

This is the first day of Floralia, a Roman festival dedicated to Flora, the Roman goddess of flowers. Decorate with flowers that you either bought or collected from your garden, or plant flowers in your yard or in a container today in her honor. Flowers represent the blessings of potential and women's mysteries. Dress in bright colors today in honor of Flora, play some music, even dance if you wish. In a bright-colored dish, make a mixture of milk and honey—Flora's favorite offering. Leave it outside for Flora in the dish or pour it out. Offer this blessing:

> Lady Flora, you bless us with your blooms,
>
> Bringing joy onto the earth as all of life resumes.
>
> Please accept this offering of lovely milk and honey
>
> As I celebrate your flowers on this day so bright and sunny.

Mickie Mueller

The Sensitive Plant

And Spring arose on the garden fair,

Like the Spirit of Love felt everywhere;

And each flower and herb on Earth's dark breast

Rose from the dreams of its wintry rest.

Percy Bysshe Shelley

April 29

Sunday

 1st ♌

2nd Quarter 5:57 am

Color of the day: Yellow
Incense of the day: Juniper

Sacred Dance and Sacred Plants

Celebrate two important events today—Pagan Tree Day and International Dance Day—in one ritual! Plant a tree or herb (preferably in the morning) and dedicate it to the associated deity. For example: chamomile for Shiva or patchouli for Hecate, and so forth.

Take into consideration your growing zone and season, then plant your tree or herb in a private spot in your garden. If you're renting, plant your tree or herb in a container. Sprinkle or carry herbs such as bay, cinnamon, and frankincense in a yellow mojo bag with a piece of tiger's eye or amber. Either play some music or listen for the rhythm of nature, and dance around your plant. Dedicate it with words like:

I give this seedling
a place to grow,

In honor of (_____) we ebb
and flow.

Dance with me (_____)
and set me free,

Grow strong little plant and
Blessed Be!"

Dance until the energy climaxes, then meditate on nature.

Kelly Proudfoot

Notes:

April 30
Monday

 2nd ♌
) v/c 10:17 am

) → ♍ 7:02 am

Color of the day: Gray
Incense of the day: Lily

A New Besom Sweeps Clean!

The besom (broom) is a powerful symbol for the witch who works magic at the center of her home. The besom may be made or acquired through purchase or gift. It's traditional to name it (as one would name a familiar) and consecrate it in a special ceremony. At the close of the ceremony, hold the besom across your heart and make a wish: legend says that it will come true. Keep the blessed besom close for seven days, then place in your sanctum sanctorum. Standing it just inside the door will prevent bad luck or evil spirits from entering.

Use your besom in ritual to cast or close a circle or to banish, cleanse, or purify, literally sweeping in or away unwanted essences. Work deosil—clockwise—to cleanse, and widdershins—counterclockwise—to banish. For spring-cleaning purposes, use a besom to "sweep finish" each room as it is cleaned.

Susan Pesznecker

NOTES:

The Fasti

*You start in April and cross to
the time of May*

*One has you as it leaves, one as
it comes*

*Since the edges of these months
are yours and defer*

*To you, either of them suits
your praises.*

*The Circus continues and the
theatre's lauded palm,*

*Let this song, too, join the
Circus spectacle.*

Ovid

May

For witches and Pagans, May marks the "height" of the year, as we see with the Beltane sabbat. This Celtic holiday is the precise opposite of Samhain (Halloween) on the Wiccan Wheel of the Year. While the beginning of November marks a descent into darkness, the beginning of May marks an ascent into light. This is a month of fertility and frivolity, sensuality and human connection, making it a good idea to reflect on sex and sexuality. What is your relationship with sex? Do you overuse or neglect your sexuality? What is your view on orientation? What are your sexual imprints from childhood? Meditating on and studying both sex and sexuality in a cross-cultural context can help you develop a more realistic, balanced, and healthy understanding of this human force of pleasure and reproduction. All too often, people choose to ignore or shutoff their sexuality or overindulge in their urges. Certainly, either side of the equation is imbalanced. This month is bright, illuminating, celebratory, and sexual. We all have the option and opportunity to positively embrace our relationship with sexuality, and May is the most ideal time for it!

Raven Digitalis

May 1
Tuesday

Beltane

2nd ♏

Color of the day: Maroon
Incense of the day: Cinnamon

Beltane Flower Charm

Let's use the language of flowers to celebrate Beltane! Create a little nosegay from garden flowers and make a charming bouquet as a gift for someone special today. Try roses for love, daisies for innocence, snapdragons for protection, carnations for health, lilac for a first love, ferns for enchantment, lavender for good luck, pansies for easing the heart, hosta leaves for devotion. Meadow sweet talks of a lovely bride, nigella says: "Kiss me quick!." Ivy is for fidelity, tulips for royalty, peonies for beauty, sweet peas for tenderness, and verbena whispers of witchcraft.

Gather your chosen flowers and tie them together with a pretty ribbon. Attach a card if you want to explain the meanings of the blossoms. You can enchant the gift with the following verse:

> Beltane flowers given from
> the heart,
>
> Are blessed with love and this
> witch's art.

Ellen Dugan

May 2
Wednesday

2nd ♏
☽ v/c 6:58 am
☽ → ♎ 10:04 pm

Color of the day: Yellow
Incense of the day: Honeysuckle

Open the Windows!

Today is truly the perfect day to remove clutter and get rid of all remnants of candle wax, cat fur, and incense from around your home! This includes making your altar neat and tidy. So, set aside a few good moments to clean the most neglected parts of your space and make room (literal and energetic) for the possibilities this allows to flourish. Take a deep breath and dive in! You'll be surprised by how much life-energy this will breathe into your next ritual or spell working. Go about your chores with an intention, trusting that the open, clear spaces you create will give rise to new adventures of various kinds, from welcome additions to your home to brilliant insights. Sprinkle a pinch of anise into the corners of each room you've cleansed to welcome in psychic vibrancy. As a finishing touch, pick wild flowers, or fragrant blossoms such as jasmine, and put them where they can be seen, smelled, and enjoyed.

Chandre Alexandre

May 3
Thursday

2nd ♎

Color of the day: Green
Incense of the day: Nutmeg

National Day of Prayer (Interfaith, USA)

The roots of this holiday go back to the 1700s, although it was not pinned down to a specific time (the first Thursday in May) until 1988. The manner of its observation, and the religions that choose to participate in it, have varied over time. The core concept is simply to encourage people to honor a higher power of their choice. For some years, the holiday was celebrated as an interfaith event. More recently, mainstream religions have predominated the event, sometimes to the point of annoying people who follow other traditions. Prayer is a widespread—nearly universal—human practice, so there is no need to have a narrow interpretation of this holiday.

Today is an ideal time for outreach. Hold a simple ritual in a safe, public place. Volunteer to read a prayer before an event. Arrange a gathering with people from diverse religions, and share a prayer from each.

Elizabeth Barrette

May 4
Friday

2nd ♎
☽ v/c 2:02 pm
☽ → ♏ 10:20 pm

Color of the day: Purple
Incense of the day: Vanilla

Chakra Charging

Tomorrow's Full Moon is a powerful time for charging your chakras with the life-giving force of nature. Find a spot in nature. Put yourself in direct contact with the Earth by placing your bare feet on the ground, or sitting directly on it. Breathe deeply. Visualize the radiant life-giving energy of the Moon, and the energy of trees, plants, and the Earth flowing up and into you through the soles of your feet, or through your root chakra. It is as if you're a plant, and the energy is facilitating your growth. Inhale. Pull this energy up through your body and around each chakra, brightening it as it's charged. Exhale and cascade excess energy from the top of your head, as though you're sitting in the midst of a fountain of light. Know that you are part of the macrocosm and that you are loved, protected, and well nourished.

Dallas Jennifer Cobb

May 5
Saturday

 Cinco de Mayo

2nd ♏

Full Moon 11:35 pm

Color of the day: Black
Incense of the day: Rue

Annoying-Neighbor Spell

This working is designed to calm quarrels between neighbors and is perfect for the Full Moon. Keep in mind that you can modify this in your own way to help calm quarrels between friends and family members if that is your issue—get creative to suit your needs! The spell will promote peace, better communication, and more compassion between the two parties.

First, acquire a paper cup and fill it with purified water. Next, put a few pinches of dirt from your own property and from your neighbor's property (ideally, from near each of your front doors, which sees a lot of foot traffic) in the cup with the water.

Next, create a mixture of any of these herbs (even if it's only two or three of them): slippery elm, yarrow, cedar, dandelion, lemongrass, clove, foxglove, vervain, and cinquefoil, and the minerals alum, sugar, and salt. These herbs and minerals are for drawing boundaries, promoting peace, increasing positive communication, and sweetening up a situation. Add a few pinches of this mixture to the water and stick it in the freezer. Sprinkle the rest of the herbs in a line between your property and theirs, and repeat:

> Boundary!
> Peace!
> Calming!
> Communication!
> Cooperation!

Raven Digitalis

NOTES:

May 6
Sunday

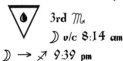

3rd ♏

☽ v/c 8:14 am

☽ → ♐ 9:39 pm

Color of the day: Gold
Incense of the day: Marigold

Ritual Shower Spell

A lot of rituals suggest you take a ritual bath beforehand, but many people prefer to take showers. Here is a way to do a ritual shower. If possible, have incense and soap of the same fragrance—lavender, sandalwood, or cedar are good. If you can't find a soap to match your incense, use plain unscented white soap. Take a stick of incense and use it to cense the bathroom. Fill the tub with warm water and get in. Wash your legs and feet, saying:

*Blessed are my legs, that walk
in the ways of the Goddess*

Wash you arms and hands, saying:

*Blessed are my arms, which do
the work of the Goddess*

Wash your torso, saying:

*Blessed is my body, formed in
the image of the Divine*

Finally, wash your face, saying:

*Blessed is my face, which shines
with the light of the Goddess."*

Rinse off, dry, and put on clean robes or clothes.

Magenta

NOTES:

May 7
Monday

 3rd ♐

Color of the day: White
Incense of the day: Narcissus

The Magic of Dew

Dew is magical. According to myth, dew was created each morning by Aurora, the goddess of the dawn. As the legend goes, Aurora would rise from the sea before sunrise and carry with her an urn filled with the morning dew. We can create our own magic with dew, especially in the spring when it's supposed to be most potent. To increase your psychic abilities, try this age-old ritual. In the early morning, moisten your finger, or a cotton ball, with dew you've collected from the grass. With this dew, anoint your forehead above the third eye. This was done by psychics long ago. To cleanse and charge a magical tool, lay the tool in the dewy grass and wipe it dry with a clean cloth. Your tool will be both cleansed and empowered. Dew is at its most powerful when it is collected at that moment between night and day, when ribbons of daylight begin to streak the horizon.

James Kambos

May 8
Tuesday

 3rd ♐
☽ v/c 9:34 pm
☽ → ♑ 10:00 pm

Color of the day: Gray
Incense of the day: Ginger

Invite Love In

We all want to love and be loved, although that may mean something different to each of us. Whether single or settled, take a moment to invite love into your heart and any other place you want it. Sprinkle rose petals on your altar, light a pink candle (for romantic love) or a red candle (for passion), or both. Then put both hands on your heart chakra and feel it open to let love in.

Light of love enfold my heart

Surround my being with sweetness—sultry, soothing, sensual, shining

A singular, plural completeness

In the form that suits me best and fits me like a glove

Fancy, funny, frolicking, flirting

Open my heart to love

Deborah Blake

May 9
Wednesday

3rd ♑

Color of the day: Yellow
Incense of the day: Bay laurel

Divination

Your divination methods can get rusty if you don't practice using them. Just like piano, to get really good at it, you need to practice. While everyone doesn't have to become a master, divination can help you to better your own position.

Once a week, say on Wednesday, set aside an hour during the day. Take out the cards, the rune stones, the mirror, the crystal ball, or whatever you use. Clear your mind for a while. Spend some quality time with your chosen method of divination. Learn something new about your method, or try something different. Explore the ways that divination can be applied to your everyday life. A cuppa' coffee and a book or two at Barnes and Noble or Borders can yield a take-home book that will get you interested again.

Boudica

May 10
Thursday

3rd ♑
☽ v/c 3:11 pm

Color of the day: Turquoise
Incense of the day: Apricot

Sacred Cedar

On the Pacific Northwest coast, the western red cedar—*Thuja plicata*—is called the "Tree of Life." Local Indian myths speak of cedar as a gift from the creator, a tree that served the local people in both practical and sacred ways. Cedar wood was used for construction, baskets, clothing, and medicine. The wood was also used to create ceremonial vessels and masks, while the shavings were burned as a rich, aromatic incense.

Create your own cedar shavings with a piece of wood and a pocket-knife, or purchase a bag of cedar shavings from a pet store. Pile loose shavings on a charcoal pellet in a small iron cauldron or other thurible and burn to release the scent. For a longer-lasting scent, combine the shavings with shaved beeswax. Cedar is associated with grounding, meditation, and protection. Use it when your do energy work and feel the connection to ancient sacred Earth.

Susan Pesznecker

May 11
Friday

 3rd ♑
☽ → ♒ 1:03 am

Color of the day: Rose
Incense of the day: Thyme

Affirmation for Self-Love

Use this spell to affirm your self-confidence and self-love, to dispel low self-esteem, and to push away self-defeating notions. Know, too, that you're never alone in feeling this way. Find comfort in understanding these thoughts and feelings are a natural part of the human condition.

Hold a piece of rose quartz in your hand, or use a piece of rose quartz jewelry that you've charged. Whenever you feel the need, hold the stone or wear the piece of jewelry and say:

I am a child of this Earth;

I realize my own true worth.

When times are tough,
I hold this stone

Reminding me I'm not alone.

If you don't have rose quartz, use amber or emerald. Of course, always seek medical care if you consistently feel down. Talking to someone is often the first step to feeling better.

Ember Grant

May 12
Saturday

 3rd ♒
4th Quarter 5:47 pm

☽ v/c 8:52 pm
Color of the day: Blue
Incense of the day: Ivy

On the Prowl

In line with the Belgium Cat Parade, use this day to prowl and release your inhibitions—within reason, of course! Tap into the feline energies and feel your true feminine nature, whether male or female. Are you repressed, oppressed, or do you unnecessarily impose restrictions on yourself? Carry a dark purple or crimson mojo bag of yarrow, hibiscus, and catnip with a piece of onyx and anointed with ylang-ylang or juniper oil. Sniff it from time to time, holding in your left hand, to release your inhibitions. Feel the courage to do and say what you feel is true to your inner self. At twilight, act like a cat and indulge in pleasure, whether sexual or otherwise. Eat a sumptuous meal, or have a glass of wine, and explore your hidden self! Engage in nocturnal activities you normally might shy away from, but be safe at the same time.

Kelly Proudfoot

May 13
Sunday
Mother's Day

 4th ♒
☽ → ♓ 7:42 am

Color of the day: Orange
Incense of the day: Frankincense

Remember the Great Mother

While we take a moment to remember all the mothers in our lives today, why not take a few minutes to remember the Great Mother Goddess, Mother of All. Find a comfortable place to sit down, if the weather permits outside is best, but you can do this inside if need be; the energy will travel where it needs to. Feel roots growing down from the base of your spine into the Earth. Allow the energy of Mother Earth to fill your roots. Now place your hands on the Earth and deliver your gift to Her, send Her love, and appreciation for all She does to sustain you. Send healing for all the harm that She's sustained. Fill your heart with joy, and send it to your Mother Earth and thank Her. Now, have a beautiful day and don't forget how blessed we all are to live upon the Earth.

Mickie Mueller

May 14
Monday

 4th ♓

Color of the day: Lavender
Incense of the day: Lily

Lily of the Valley Spell

Lily of the valley is an old-fashioned, enchanting faerie flower. Its blossom is sweetly scented and has the ability to lift our spirits and bring cheer into any room where it's placed. Today let's work with the energies of the waning Moon and the power of this flower and conjure up a happiness spell. Tuck a few stems of the flower into a vase and say:

Lily of the valley tiny though it may be,

Has the power to remove negativity.

May the waning Moon banish all sadness around here,

While this faerie flower brings cheer to those I hold dear.

Allow the flowers to work their magic until they begin to fade. Then gently return them to nature.

Ellen Dugan

May 15
Tuesday

 4th ♓
♈ v/c 7:59 am
☽ → ♈ 5:45 pm

Color of the day: Red
Incense of the day: Ylang-ylang

Flower Spell

May flowers are very potent in spell working. Knowing the "language" of flowers is a simple method of putting our intentions before the Universe as a signal for the world to meet our needs. Growing your own flowers is very satisfying, but not necessary for this spell. You can walk through the woods picking wild flowers, or select a bouquet from a florist shop. Small bouquets were known as Tussie Mussies and could be used to send specific messages. Although we are most familiar with the meanings of roses, there are many other floras that can be used to specify our needs and wants in spell working. For those with access to a computer, a search for "Language of Flowers" will bring up a number of excellent sites to help you decide which flowers or plants can be used in your own specific spell. Your local library can also provide you with books and articles to help in this search for spell-working tools.

Paniteowl

May 16
Wednesday

 4th ♈

Color of the day: Brown
Incense of the day: Lilac

A Garden Protection Spell

The planting season is in full swing, and now is the time to protect your garden from any pests. This spell will surround your garden with a protective aura. The spell is contained in the following verse. On a May eve, when the shadows of night lie upon the land, in a firm voice, announce this command:

By the powers of all the directions—east, west, north and south—I demand that all pests, be cast out!

Conclude the ritual by holding a twig in your power hand, and as you do so, turn clockwise to seal your garden with a shield of protective energy.

Finally, break the twig in two and throw it in a direction away from your garden. All animals—both beast and fowl—have witnessed your magical decree. Now, rest easy.

James Kambos

May 17
Thursday

 4th ♈
♈ v/c 5:44 pm

Color of the day: Crimson
Incense of the day: Myrrh

Dea Dia Invocation

Call on Dea Dia, the Roman god-dess of agriculture, the sky, and the Earth, to help plough your (meta-phorical) fields and make way for positive new growth in your life.

As the Sun rises, assemble a small offering of incense, fruit, and red wine. Place it on your altar, or outside on the ground or a small table. Light the incense and say:

Dea Dia, great goddess, I call on you, and I offer you these gifts!

Goddess of earth and sky, of plough and field, of mud and dirt, vibrant light, and upward growth, I call on you!

Guide me to release the old so that the new may enter.

Help me to prepare the soil of my soul.

Assist me in sowing beautiful new conditions in my life!

From the deepest depths of my heart, I thank you!

Tess Whitehurst

May 18
Friday

 4th ♈
☽ → ♉ 6:03 am

Color of the day: Coral
Incense of the day: Orchid

Old Clothes Spell

Do you have a piece of clothing that you dearly love, but it's become unwearable? Want to keep the memories and good vibes? Here's how. You need an item of new cloth-ing similar to the old one, for exam-ple, a new sweater for an old one. Put on the new clothing, then, if possible, put the old clothing over it, sand-wiching the new one between the old and yourself. Wear it, and recall your feelings for the clothing. If you can't put the old clothing on over the new, find some way to wrap it around your body. A sweater or shirt can be draped over the shoulders; a pair of pants can be tied around your waist by the legs. For shoes, wear one of the old ones on one foot, and one of the new ones on the other, then, swap them around. This will capture some of the aura of the old item.

Magenta

May 19
Saturday

 4th ♉

Color of the day: Black
Incense of the day: Pine

The hidden Door

For a spell caster, the mind is the most important tool. Therefore, it helps to practice mental exercises to develop your mind and its skills as much as possible. With a lack of stimulation, it's easy to become bored, and bored minds tend to wander. When you are stuck waiting for a long time, practice this mental exercise.

Imagine yourself facing a door. Focus on its details—the material, the knob, anything else that catches your fancy. Silently say:

The spirit cannot be caged;
Time has no roof and no floor.
The mind cannot be captured;
Walk free through the hidden door.

Visualize opening the door and stepping through with one foot. Keep the other foot firmly planted where you are. In this way, you can entertain yourself in the privacy of your own mind, while remaining aware of what happens around you.

Elizabeth Barrette

May 20
Sunday

 4th ♉
☽ v/c 8:35 am
☉ → ♊ 11:16 am
☽ → ♊ 7:05 pm
New Moon 7:47 pm

Color of the day: Yellow
Incense of the day: Hydrangea

Growing-Time Spell

The Sun moves into Gemini, a sign of duality. Associated with the element of Air; the anatomy of hands, arms, and lungs; and the characteristics of sociable, talkative, and responsive, Gemini is closely associated with the exchange of ideas, communication, and trade. Invite a few friends to gather in the evening, and ask each one to bring some seeds with them, either seeds harvested from their garden last year, or a packet of seeds that they have purchased. Have people sit in a small circle and call in the directions.

North, east, south, and west
Circle us and do your best

Protect us all in sacred space

Bless these people,
bless this space.

Let everyone introduce their seeds, telling what they like about the plant, or a story about it in their garden.

Provide small pieces of paper so everyone can take a few seeds from each packet, and wrap them separately to take home.

> We exchange ideas, and exchange seeds, we give freely and we receive,
>
> With your hands, plant these seeds, to honor your lungs and the air we breathe,
>
> Seeds of wisdom, shared with friends, with these seeds the cycle begins again.

Dallas Jennifer Cobb

NOTES:

May 21
Monday

1st ♊

Color of the day: Gray
Incense of the day: Rosemary

What's Ganesha Got to Do with It?

With the Sun in Gemini, we get the guidance of an Air sign that offers mirth, cleverness, and ingenuity on the one hand, and flightiness, skepticism, and a rueful mood on the other. To make the most of both worlds and find the usefulness in sometimes difficult characteristics or traits, you might wish to offer prayers to Lord Ganesha.

This Hindu elephant-headed god has the uncanny ability to place in our paths just what we need to overcome on the road to greater success. Present this playful and intense son of Shiva and Parvati—a lover of sweets—with delicious goodies as you ask for the strength and courage to maneuver through life's challenges. Of particular poignancy today are endeavors of the intellect that require focus, discernment, clarity, and faculties of the higher mind. Once you have made your offering and asked for guidance or support, be sure to taste and share the sweets you have placed at Ganesha's feet as a sign of your willingness to take in his blessing.

Chandra Alexandre

May 22
Tuesday

 1st ♊

☽ v/c 6:51 pm

Color of the day: Red
Incense of the day: Basil

Garden Blessing

Obtain some seeds or starter plants and prepare a place for them to grow. As you plant them, visualize them growing strong and healthy. This can be for a vegetable, flower, or herb garden—or all of these. Use for containers or permanent gardens. Tuesday is ruled by Mars, god of war. Take advantage of this energy to infuse your plants with strength. Place a garnet or piece of bloodstone near the plants.

Bless this garden,
plants be strong;

Bless this garden,
living long.

May I reap the fruits I sow,
Bountiful, my garden grow.

Ember Grant

May 23
Wednesday

 1st ♊

☽ → ♋ 7:31 am

Color of the day: Brown
Incense of the day: Marjoram

Bay Leaf Vision

Bay leaves are often used as a cooking spice; it can just as easily be used in witchcraft. Focusing on bay leaves, we are reminded of the Oracles of Delphi. These ancient Greek prophetesses are said to have chewed on bay leaves as part of their oracular work. We can utilize the essence of this practice in our own lives in a simple way (or a complex manner, depending on how deep one wishes to take their oracular work). When you wish to gain insight or clarity into a situation, take six bay leaves and brew them as a tea. When steeped, put yourself in a meditative state of mind for the duration of the cup of tea. While you sip the tea, simultaneously chew on the moist bay leaves (you don't need to swallow them) and contemplate the issue you need insight on. You may be surprised by the insight you gain, especially if you practice this working on numerous occasions over time!

Raven Digitalis

May 24
Thursday

1st ♋

Color of the day: Green
Incense of the day: Clove

Prosperity

Thursdays are great days to do prosperity work. Of course, prosperity means different things to different people. For some, it means having enough money to survive until another day. For others, it means being able to indulge your deepest desires. Whatever prosperity means to you, here is a simple spell to encourage it. Light a green candle. Take a pile of coins (pennies, nickels, it doesn't matter what kind) and hold them in your left hand, then slowly spill them into your right hand, and back again, saying the following:

> *Money grows and money flows*
>
> *From one hand to another*
>
> *Prosperity flow into my life*
>
> *And grant me what I need*
>
> *So mote it be*

Deborah Blake

May 25
Friday

1st ♋
☽ v/c 10:34 am
☽ → ♌ 6:11 pm

Color of the day: White
Incense of the day: Alder

Romantic Evening Love Spell

Sometimes couples or longtime companions can find some of the spark lacking in their relationship. An answer to that is the romantic evening love spell.

First you need intent. Set a time for your romantic interlude. Then, set your space. If it is to be dinner, movie, and conversation, set up the living room for a close encounter. Put out some romantic snack food—chocolate, strawberries, and your favorite drinks. Pick a movie that both of you enjoy.

Then comes the fun. Plan on close contact, have the bedroom prepared, or if you want to really get into it, make sure there are pillows and sheets in the living room for that "spur of the moment" encounter.

Like any good spell, planning quality time with each other requires intent, the right ingredients and a little spark of the love magic to kindle the passion.

Boudica

May 26
Saturday

 1st ♌

Color of the day: Brown
Incense of the day: Patchouli

Honoring Stones

Stones are of the Earth. They are created, demolished, and rebirthed in geological cycles that last millions of years. Stones are the Earth's true elders: use them to create the ultimate green altar.

Earth: Metamorphic stones are created through time and pressure. A marble or granite stone will represent enduring strength on your altar.

Air: Pumice is ejected through volcanic action into the air. Once cooled, it's feather light and honeycombed with minuscule air pockets.

Fire: At one time or another, all stones are shaped by fire, whether through volcanic eruption or by heat and pressure deep below Earth's surface. Look for a piece of dense, black basalt, or a bit of pahoehoe lava.

Water: Petrified wood is formed of wood, water, and time. Set a piece on your altar to invoke water's transformation.

Spirit: A pure quartz crystal—beautiful, hard, and capable of conducting energy—speaks of the Earth's mystery and power.

Susan Pesznecker

May 27
Sunday

Shavuot

 1st ♌
☽ v/c 7:54 pm

Color of the day: Orange
Incense of the day: Heliotrope

Star of the Show Spell

Yes, you may be shy. Still, there will be certain situations during which you will want to be the star of the show, or to supercharge your visibility and reputation. Today's the perfect day to create a charm to help you do just that. As the Sun rises, face east. Light a red or orange candle. Warm a pyrite with the flame as you chant:

I am the star,
I am the star,
I am the star.

Place the pyrite in a red flannel bag. Add a stick of cinnamon, a dried chili pepper, and a piece of fresh ginger. Say:

I burn bright,
I burn bright,
I burn bright.

Tie the bag closed with gold ribbon. Gently warm the bag with the flame; then hold it to your heart. The next time you want to be the star, carry the charm or place it near a picture of yourself.

Tess Whitehurst

May 28
Monday

Memorial Day (observed)

1st ♌

☽ → ♍ 2:06 am

2nd Quarter 4:16 pm

Color of the day: Ivory
Incense of the day: Clary sage

Flag Spell

Memorial Day in the USA is a time to remember those who gave their lives so that we may live. The traditional flying of the "Red, White, and Blue" is part of the American scene; however, other flags are available that serve as well. Each branch of the Armed Forces has its own flag. You can honor a family member who served under a particular flag by including that flag in your display. Whether you fly the flag outdoors or use the small flags in an arrangement on your table, you are doing a spell working when you bring these people to the forefront of your mind. Honoring your ancestors by including flags of their countries increases the potency of this special Memorial Day. Combining flags and flowers sends a message of gratitude to those who have gone before us. Simple acknowledgement, in the language of flags and flowers, can be one of the most satisfying methods to heal the heartbreak of loss.

Paniteowl

May 29
Tuesday

2nd ♍

Color of the day: White
Incense of the day: Cedar

Oak Apple Day Magical Ink

Today is Oak Apple Day. Here is a medieval ink you can make from oak apples that will add power to your spells or book of shadows. An oak apple is also known as an oak gall, a small round growth that appears on oak branches. Crush several oak galls and boil them for about 5 minutes, in just enough water to cover them. While they cool, cover 13 rusty iron nails in a dish of vinegar for several hours. When cool, pour the oak gall water through cheesecloth or a coffee filter, and combine the water with the rusty nail vinegar. You may add some ash to darken it if needed and gum arabic as a binder; store in an airtight container. You can enchant your ink with the following:

> *This oak apple ink,*
> *I fill with my might,*
>
> *Recording with power,*
> *every word that I write.*

Mickie Mueller

May 30
Wednesday

 2nd ♏
☽ v/c 1:50 am
☽ → ♎ 6:46 am

Color of the day: White
Incense of the day: Lavender

Celebrate Intuition with Joan of Arc

Pay homage to Joan of Arc today, her feast day. Meditate on her trials and tribulations. Think about how she held fast to her beliefs in such malicious times. Make a banner for her with symbols of her passion, dedication, and courage. (Don't be discouraged by the Christian implications—her spirit transcends all that!)

Anoint a blue candle with clove oil, and light it for her. Toast to her triumph over evil with a glass of wine, and think of women in your sphere who are likewise struggling against adversity. Swear an oath to assist your sisters and stand beside them.

Burn herbs, such as lavender, lemongrass, and yarrow. Take in the scent and go into a trance. Listen to the voice of your Higher Self. What messages do you receive? How have you been neglecting your soul's urge? Make plans to set things right and to trust your intuition.

Kelly Proudfoot

May 31
Thursday

 2nd ♎
☽ v/c 9:31 pm

Color of the day: Purple
Incense of the day: Balsam

honor the Muse

The last day of the month has traditionally been dedicated to chthonic aspects of goddess, to those who possess intimate knowledge of the transformational process. In resonance with these powers, bring in your ability to call from the depths of your being the sweet song of your soul through music, voice, art, movement, or other creative endeavors. Find a time today to express your muse. Be willing to return to childhood toys (crayons, silly putty, play dough, finger paints, and so on), letting the full expression of who you are be available as you engage the whim of the moment. Listen to the wisdom that comes through your exploration, and be willing to share your creativity with others. In gratitude for the experience, make an offering to the muse of your heart and dedicate your creation to someone or something meaningful to you. If you wish, leave an apple at a crossroads to affirm the benefits and learnings you've attained and to invite the seeds of fruitful attainment to be planted for others.

Chandra Alexandre

The Roman poet Ovid provides two etymologies for June's name in his poem "The Fasti." The first is that the month is named after the Roman goddess Juno, wife of Jupiter and the patroness of weddings and marriage. That is a nice tie-in, because June is known as the month for weddings. The second is that the name comes from the Latin word *iuniores*, meaning "younger ones," as opposed to *maiores*, meaning "elders," for which May is named. The birthstone is the pearl, or sometimes alexandrite or moonstone. The flower associated with the month is the rose, and roses tend to be abundant and blooming in June in the Northern Hemisphere. The Summer Solstice, usually on June 21 or 22, is also referred to as Midsummer. In the Northern Hemisphere, the beginning of the meteorological summer is June 1st; in the Southern Hemisphere, June 1st the beginning of the meteorological winter.

Magenta

June 1
Friday

2nd ♎

☽ → ♏ 8:31 am

Color of the day: Rose
Incense of the day: Mint

A Wedding Ring Spell

June is the month of weddings, and this spell offers a perfect way to enchant a pair of wedding rings. This blessing could also be used if you wish to renew your commit-ment. If possible, perform this ritual as a couple. Begin by tying the rings together with a pink ribbon. Light a pink candle and pass the rings above the flame, then place them in front of the candle. Together say:

> Let this candle burn, with the warmth of the Sun,
>
> As these rings are bound, we are one.
>
> To you I give my heart and hand,
>
> For you only, I'll wear this wedding band.

Let the candle burn itself out. Keep the rings tied together and wrap them in a piece of pretty fabric. A lace handkerchief that's a family heir-loom would work well. On the eve-ning before you wed, untie the rings. Blessed be!

James Kambos

June 2
Saturday

2nd ♏

Color of the day: Indigo
Incense of the day: Magnolia

Rose Petal Spell

I like to sprinkle a circle of fresh rose petals on the grass when I cast spells in my magical garden. Here is my circle-casting spell for you to try this summer:

> Elements four gather round as I call you near,
>
> Earth, Air, Fire and Water, come join with me here.
>
> Surround me with your powers and circle around,
>
> Only enchantment and joy will ever be found.
>
> My circle is cast, as above, now so below,
>
> By the Sun, the Moon, and stars, this circle will hold.

To release the circle, use this verse:

> Water, Fire, Air, and Earth, elements four I now release,
>
> With my love and thanks for each of your strengths, now depart in peace.

Ellen Dugan

June 3
Sunday

2nd ♏

☽ v/c 5:29 am

☽ → ♐ 8:32 am

Color of the day: Amber
Incense of the day: Juniper

Roman Festival of Bellona

Bellona is the female embodiment of Roman military virtue. Celebrated on June 3rd, she is usually depicted as a woman in military garb. In ancient Rome, however, it was not the woman's place to be a warrior. But other cultures have shown us women do have a place in society as a warrior.

Take time to contemplate our female warriors: military and peace officers—any woman who stands for justice and who fights for the rights of the individual. They wear many different uniforms. The most important lesson we've learned is that a woman's place is anywhere a woman wants to be. If we want to explore and learn, we can be the warriors society needs; a balance between the force needed and the wisdom to know when to stop and use our heads. We are the embodiment of military virtue—know when to fight and when to make peace.

Boudica

History & Lore of the Pearl

The pearl holds a special place of honor among gems. It is the oldest-known gem, and for a long time, it was also considered the most valuable. In ancient Persia, pearls were "worth their weight in gold." Some historians believe Julius Caesar invaded Britain in 55 BC to obtain freshwater pearls. Pearls symbolized the Moon to ancients, who believed them to be magical, as well. The Mayan and Aztec people prized pearls for their magical power, and when explorers to the New World returned to their own countries, they referred to places where the Mayan and Aztecs lived as "the lands where pearls come from." In the thirteenth and fourteenth centuries, most European counties had laws about who could and could not wear pearls. People of rank could wear them, while teachers and lawyers, who didn't have a rank, could not.

Lee Obrien

June 4
Monday

 2nd ♐
𝔉ull Moon 7:12 am

Color of the day: Lavender
Incense of the day: Lily

Eclipse Magic

Today is a Full Moon and a partial lunar eclipse. A lunar eclipse occurs when Earth is between the Sun and Moon, causing Earth's shadow to be cast over the Moon. This eclipse will be visible from most of Asia, Australia, the Pacific Ocean, and the northwestern Americas.

Eclipses are times of potent magics and mysteries. Celebrate the eclipsed Full Moon by spending a full day honoring our favorite satellite. Wear silver or white. Divide your day into eight sections—one for each of the lunar phases: new, waxing quarter, waxing half, waxing gibbous, full, waning gibbous, waning half, waning quarter, and new again. At each section, meditate on the lunar phase, keeping the Moon on your mind.

Arrange the day so you're available at the moment of Full Moon and eclipse. Reaching skyward, draw down the lunar energies. This is an excellent time to charge water, oils, or other spell materials, as well as to bless and charge tools.

The moment of maximum eclipse is possibly the most powerful time for writing in your Book of Shadows. Working under eclipsed moonlight, use a special pen to capture the lunar energies, literally "writing down the Moon" into your own spell and ritual craft.

Susan Pesznecker

NOTES:

June 5
Tuesday

3rd ♐

☽ v/c 1:08 am

☽ → ♑ 8:31 am

Color of the day: Red
Incense of the day: Cinnamon

A Sacred Cigarette?

I personally advocate freedom from all forms of addiction. That having been said, it should be known that tobacco can and should be used in a sacred manner; this is especially pertinent for those living in the Americas whose ancestors utilized the tobacco plant's sacred medicine for both physical and metaphysical uses. As a small tribute to the ancestors and the elements (and only if you are eighteen or older, of course), acquire an all-natural, organic cigarette, or pipe tobacco. When lit, draw the smoke into your mouth without inhaling. When the smoke is in your mouth, turn in a clockwise direction to the north, east, south, and west, blowing a puff of smoke to the elements. Do the same to the ground beneath you and the sky above you. Next, blow puffs of pure tobacco smoke to the spirits of the land around you, to the ancestors, and to any deities you wish to give thanks to. Finish by leaving offerings of tobacco in the area around you.

Raven Digitalis

June 6
Wednesday

3rd ♑

Color of the day: Topaz
Incense of the day: Lavender

Early Morning Elements

Take extra time in the morning to connect with the elements and the Pagan path.

I honor the east,
with the rising Sun,

The breath of the Goddess,
the ancient one,

I honor the south,
and sacred fire,

The Sun brings warmth,
passion and desire,

I honor the west,
the ancient waters,

The spirit of Crone, Mother,
and Daughter,

I honor the north,
our Mother Earth,

The eternal cycle of life,
death and rebirth,

Safe within this sacred sphere,

Protected and loved,
I dwell here.

Dallas Jennifer Cobb

June 7
Thursday

3rd ♑
) v/c 8:38 am
) → ♒ 10:17 am

Color of the day: Green
Incense of the day: Jasmine

Protection for hearth and home

On this day in ancient Rome, Vesta, the goddess of hearth and fire, was celebrated at Vestalia. The inner sanctum of her temple was opened for women to offer sacrifices.

Build a fire, in either your fireplace or a cauldron. Then, eat your evening meal beside it, with or without your family and/or friends. Make an incense of rosemary, rose, and violet and throw it into the fire as an offering. Say aloud:

> Blessed Vesta, goddess of the
> hearth and fire, I ask for your
> protection. Please partake in
> this meal, in honor of your
> shining light. Watch over my
> home, bring peace to all who
> enter and banish those who
> wish me harm. So mote it be!

Throw another handful of the incense into the fire and see your home permeated with white light. Know that you and your home are protected. Interpret the future omens of the flames of the fire.

Kelly Proudfoot

June 8
Friday

3rd ♒
Color of the day: White
Incense of the day: Rose

Send It Forward

Traditionally, June 8 is a day to foretell future weather conditions. Folklore from England, France, and America all concur that if it rains on June 8, it will also rain on the harvest. Using this belief that somehow what happens on this day affects the future, you can focus the energies of this day to manifest what you want in the future. Upon waking, decide what you want to see manifest by the harvest time. Write it down and carry it with you, thinking of it many times today, if you can do anything towards that end, all the better, make plans, make a phone call, send an e-mail in regard to your plans. Before the sun goes down, go outside and light a stick of your favorite incense, concentrate on what you want as you watch the smoke rise into the June 8th sky, and let it manifest with the harvest.

Mickie Mueller

June 9
Saturday

3rd ♒

☽ v/c 2:33 pm

☽ → ♓ 3:22 pm

Color of the day: Black
Incense of the day: Sage

Love Spell

Three red candles and a bouquet of red roses help to focus the energy of this spell. As you light the candles and arrange the flowers, chant with a firm voice:

Earth and Air, Water and Fire, please bring me my heart's desire.

True of heart and fair of face, near to me will find a place.

Warm and loving everlasting, for my same species I am casting.

This last line was added to an old spell because a friend of mine did a working and wound up with a true, loyal, beautiful dog!

Paniteowl

June 10
Sunday

3rd ♓

Color of the day: Amber
Incense of the day: Eucalyptus

Health and Energy Spell

Each of the four classical elements plays an important role in keeping us healthy. We eat of the Earth, we breathe the air, our bodies must keep a certain temperature, and we must drink water. In addition, these elements correspond to our flesh and bones, breath, blood, and organs—all connected. We are made up of these sacred elements.

Face each direction and speak the following words:

North: Earth nourish my body

East: Air nourish my mind

South: Fire energize

West: Water revitalize

Repeat as needed, visualizing each element blessing you with its qualities.

Ember Grant

June 11
Monday

3rd ♓
☽ v/c 6:41 am

4th Quarter 6:41 am

Color of the day: Ivory
Incense of the day: Hyssop

King Kamehameha Day

King Kamehameha was the first monarch to unite the Kingdom of Hawaii. Established in 1871, this holiday remains popular in Hawaii today. Early celebrations included carnivals, fairs, and foot and horse races. Today, floral parades and hula competitions also appear. Hula is the sacred dance of Hawaii; its rhythms and motions all have specific meanings. Many hula dances tell stories from Hawaiian mythology. By practicing this sacred dance, people can grow closer to the islands and their guardian spirits. Books, videos, and other resources illustrate the beauty of hula so that you can appreciate it even if you can't watch a performance in person. Today is a good day to study hula or to read about the gods and goddesses of Hawaii. You might also enjoy exploring the Hawaiian language—one of the few indigenous languages to have a modern resurgence.

Elizabeth Barrette

June 12
Tuesday

4th ♓
☽ → ♈ 12:21 am

Color of the day: Red
Incense of the day: Geranium

Increase Energy

As the Summer Solstice approaches, we shift gears from the planting energy of spring to the growth energy of summer. The kids are out of school, or nearly so; we're planning vacations and barbecues, and trying to keep up with the yard and garden. All of which is great—but takes a lot of energy. Luckily, the summer brings with it the abundant energy of the blossoming Earth, so we can tap into nature's bounty for a little extra energy for ourselves. Sit outside in the sunshine if you can, or by an open window. Hold a flower (or a whole bunch) in your hands and say:

> Summer Sun,
>
> summer flower
>
> Grant me energy,
>
> strength, and power

Deborah Blake

June 13
Wednesday

4th ♈
☽ v/c 11:09 pm

Color of the day: White
Incense of the day: Honeysuckle

Coconut Cleansing Bath for Beauty and Inner Peace

This day is dedicated to Hina, the Polynesian manifestation of the Great Goddess. It's the perfect time to invoke her help with a beautifying bath that cleanses body, mind, and spirit. After dark, draw a bath in a candlelit bathroom. Add two cups of coconut milk and ½ cup sea salt. Place a moonstone in the water. Hold your hands over the water and say:

Hina, radiant and beautiful Goddess, I call on you.

Please infuse this water with peaceful and healing vibrations.

May it purify and bless me in all ways so that my true beauty may be revealed,

And so I, like you, may shine my light with clarity and joy.

For this I thank you with all my heart!

Tess Whitehurst

June 14
Thursday
Flag Day

4th ♈
☽ → ♉ 12:22 pm

Color of the day: Turquoise
Incense of the day: Nutmeg

The Gift of Life

Today is Flag Day and World Blood Donor Day; it would be patriotic to go and give blood. Before you go, make sure you're in good health and dedicate your generous act to Jupiter—Lord of the Heavens. Consecrate incense made of dragonsblood, red rose, and juniper to him and burn it in your cauldron while asking him for a boost to your health—for your sake as well as for others.

In your left hand, hold a piece of bloodstone over the smoke and imagine the strength instilling its powers into the stone. Hold it in your left hand when you go to give blood, to keep your energy levels up. When you get home, burn a red candle anointed with rosemary oil and meditate on your blood rejuvenating itself.

Think about the life who will benefit and send out positive energy to that person—whoever it is.

Kelly Proudfoot

June 15
Friday

4th ♉

Color of the day: Purple
Incense of the day: Cypress

Honeysuckle Spell

Honeysuckle, also known as woodbine, has many magical properties, such as promoting prosperity and protection. Since we have a waning Moon today, let's work with the honeysuckle to boost your psychic protection. Gather a few blossoms of the honeysuckle and a few green leaves. Carry them with you or tuck the flowers into a tiny vase and keep it in your home or at your desk at work. Here is a verse to enchant the flowers.

> Woodbine, surround me with your grounding energy,
>
> Protect and guard my psychic sensitivity.
>
> By the sweet scent of the honeysuckle's, blossoms and leaves,
>
> I am shielded from draining tactics and energy thieves.

Allow the flowers to work their magic until they begin to fade. Then neatly return them to nature.

Ellen Dugan

June 16
Saturday

4th ♉
☽ v/c 8:09 am

Color of the day: Brown
Incense of the day: Sandalwood

Eradicate False Limitations Spell

When we're held back by our fears, we unintentionally limit the opportunities available to us. Use this spell today to help free yourself from ingrained responses and negative thoughts or habits that limit your creative expression and true nature.

First, make a simple drawing of a house. This represents your soul.

Now, pause and meditate on the limitations you face every day, whether self-imposed or otherwise. Draw in fences, furniture, walls—any objects that stand for limitations you create or experience within and around you. Name your challenges.

Next, meditate on what you truly want to have. In your mind's eye, bring order and a sense of purpose to objects that block you. Allow texture, smell, color, and the vibrancy of the senses to complete the inner picture.

When you're ready, open your eyes and burn the drawing you made, releasing all that holds you back.

Chandra Alexandre

June 17
Sunday
Father's Day

4th ♉
☽ → ♊ 1:24 am

Color of the day: Yellow
Incense of the day: Marigold

A Simple Protection Spell

This spell requires several lengths of cloth, or shawls, or large scarves, etc. While in a private place, like your bedroom, remove your clothes and then bathe or shower. Light a white candle and place it before your favorite representation of the Mother Goddess. Take the various cloths and bless them by Water and Earth, Fire, and Air. Chant:

> *Goddess be with me,*
> *Goddess protect me.*

Then, begin wrapping cloths around your body. Continue chanting and wrapping yourself until your body, including your feet and head are covered. When you are completely covered, chant three more times, then take a few deep breaths, and feel yourself wrapped in the protection of the Goddess. Slowly unwrap yourself, then blow out the candle. Carefully fold and put away the cloths. Wear one or two of them whenever you feel the need for protection—every day if you wish.

Magenta

June 18
Monday

4th ♊

Color of the day: Silver
Incense of the day: Clary sage

Sacrificing the Drama Llamas

One of my coven sisters is emphatic about the need to sacrifice personal "Drama Llamas" before public spiritual or social gatherings. Though the term is humorous, the necessity is grand! Because the Midsummer sabbat is coming up, you may wish to bring your focus to the drama and social silliness that surrounds your life. Keep in mind that "drama" is not a one-sided phenomenon: even the most "anti-drama" person can be dependent on gossip and the emotional roller coaster. To help dismiss socio-emotional silliness from your life, gather fresh weeds from your garden or a friend's. Weeds, in this case, represent the mass spreading of unwanted energy. Twist, tie, and bind these weeds into llama-shaped figures (they don't have to look accurate!) and dub them "Drama Llamas." Focus on all the drama in your life, and let them dry until Midsummer so you can cast them into the bonfire. If a fire is not available, drop these little buggers into flowing water to cast them away from your life!

Raven Digitalis

June 19
Tuesday

4th ♊

☽ v/c 11:02 am

New Moon 11:02 am

☽ → ♋ 1:34 pm

Color of the day: Maroon
Incense of the day: Bayberry

String Manifestation

New Moon is a good time to practice drawing, attracting, and manifestation magic. This string spell will facilitate focus to bring what you want into existence. You need a pen, some paper, a string three to four feet long, and a small table. Sit at the table and visualize what you want to manifest. See it in your mind's eye in as much detail as possible. Condense your visualization into one word. It could be the name of a person, place, or thing, or a spiritual attribute. Write this word on the paper. Fold the paper in half, and tie one end of the string around the paper. Holding one end of the string, throw the paper end away from you, over the edge of the table.

Slowly spool the string in, and drawing the paper toward you, incant:

I bring (fill in) toward me,

It comes near (draw paper up over the edge of the table).

*I pull it toward me,
and bring it here.*

I manifest all that I need,

If Goddess is willing,

So mote it be.

Do this often to maintain focus on what you desire, and remember, let go of your time line. The Goddess will provide.

Dallas Jennifer Cobb

NOTES:

June 20
Wednesday

Litha – Summer Solstice

 1st ♋
☉ → ♋ 7:09 pm

Color of the day: Brown
Incense of the day: Bay laurel

A Dream–Come–True Spell

Today, rise before sunup and watch that moment when the Sun rises. In your mind's eye, see the Sun ride his golden chariot across the sky to the pinnacle of his power, before he turns the cycle of time toward autumn. Surround yourself with solar power symbols to draw abundance to you. Light three candles on your altar—green for growth, orange for wealth/vitality, and yellow for mental clarity. Before them, in simple ceremony, place the Sun card from the tarot. Wear a piece of gold jewelry today and dream an impossible dream. Mimic the Sun and reach the height of your own power. Take steps to achieve a goal you once thought was impossible. As evening approaches, sit outdoors and let the shadows of dusk draw around you. Think how it must have been when the power of the Sun blessed a young Earth with its very first summer. Let that power flow through you as you make your dream come true.

James Kambos

June 21
Thursday

 1st ♋
☽ v/c 12:48 pm
☽ → ♌ 11:47 pm

Color of the day: White
Incense of the day: Clove

Magical Oil for Prosperity

Grow your business with Better Business Oil. There are variations on this oil, but a very basic mix is sunflower oil, cinnamon oil (just a little), bayberry oil, and some honey. Add a few small pieces of iron pyrite to the mix, maybe a little green food color to make the oil the color of money. The sunflower oil is for success, honey is a basic attractant, cinnamon oil is an accelerant, and bayberry is for increasing money.

Use this oil to anoint candles for money spells and to scent your work area. Wipe a little on the surface of your work area (always test first). Use a spell bag in which you place a silver coin, a piece of iron pyrite, an almond, and something that represents your business. If you don't have anything physical, write your business name on a piece of parchment or paper and place in it the bag.

Boudica

June 22
Friday

 1st ♌

Color of the day: Rose
Incense of the day: Vanilla

Mini-Witch Bottle

Witch bottles are typically filled with sharp objects and protective herbs and buried on one's property to draw and trap negative energies or entities. Alas: It's hard to bury a large jar outside your home if you live in a concrete-surfaced apartment complex. The solution: a mini witch bottle. You'll need:

> a small screw-top bottle
>
> 2–3 thumbtacks
>
> 2–3 straight pins
>
> a bit of red thread
>
> a spoonful of red wine
>
> some rosemary

Place the ingredients in the bottle during the waning to Dark Moon phase, which is an optimal time for wardings and banishings. Negative energies are stuck by the pins, tangled in the thread, and drowned in the wine, while the rosemary anchors the energies and sends them away. Bury the bottle outside or hide it within your home, incanting:

Tiny bottle, pins and tacks,

Hidden safe to watch my back:

Protect my home from enemies,

This is my will—so mote it be!

Susan Pesznecker

Notes:

June 23
Saturday

1st ♌
☽ v/c 6:26 pm

Color of the day: Gray
Incense of the day: Rue

Protection from Accidents

When we're distracted, full of worry, impatient, or otherwise not calm and focused, we may find ourselves in conflict with the overall harmony of life. In these times, accidents happen more frequently to remind us of what's important. In order to help protect yourself from needing harsh reminders, affirm your commitment to the work of moving beyond the ego's encumbrances. When you wake up in the morning, make the following affirmations in front of a mirror: "I am good enough." "I am worthy." "I am perfect." Then, visualize being wrapped in a beautiful blanket in which you feel warm, loved, held, content and honored. Let this experience sink in. Enjoy your day!

Chandra Alexandre

June 24
Sunday

1st ♌
☽ → ♍ 7:42 am

Color of the day: Orange
Incense of the day: Almond

Friendship Spell

Many significant relationships are about love and sex, but friendship is important, too. Don't wait for someone to find you. Be a friend someone would like to have.

Be aware of those people with whom you work, socialize, or attend classes. This is a good basis to start building a friendship because you already know there is a common interest. Plan an event! It can be as simple as suggesting a group of people you know go out to dinner together, or go to a movie. It doesn't take a great deal of effort to be a "social director" for any group, just the willingness to make suggestions and then follow through. Starting to bring people together is easier than one may think. As you get to know people better, you can then plan to invite someone to your home for a dinner, or an informal "order in" night. The important thing is to put your best foot forward and by your actions, give people a reason to befriend you.

Paniteowl

June 25
Monday

 1st ♍

Color of the day: Gray
Incense of the day: Neroli

Travel Spell

Find two ordinary, small stones in your yard. After you cleanse them with water, use them in this spell for a safe journey.

Put the stones on your altar. Light two white candles and place one on each side of the stones. Visualize the stones as guides—one to carry with you and one you'll leave at home. They are connected to help ensure a hassle-free journey and to return safely home. This is why it's important these stones come from the place where you live—ideally, your yard. Use this chant to empower the stones:

> Travel without trouble, travel without harm,
>
> Make this journey safe and fun, I activate this charm.
>
> Guide each step along my way, carefree every night and day.
>
> Success and good will where I stay, then home again,
>
> Ills kept at bay.

Ember Grant

June 26
Tuesday

 1st ♍

☽ v/c 6:53 am

☽ → ♎ 1:15 pm

2nd Quarter 11:30 pm

Color of the day: Black
Incense of the day: Ylang-ylang

Front Door Blessing

Doors, especially front doors, are magical things. Do this ritual to bless and protect your home and to call opportunity, abundance, and blessings of all forms into your life.

First, perform simple maintenance to the front door area as necessary to create a sparkling and vibrant appearance and feeling. For example, you might get a new doormat, oil the hinges, and replace an ailing plant. Or perhaps all you need to do is sweep the doorstep.

Then, fill a clean bucket with warm water. Over the bucket, use your hands to lightly crush a handful of fresh basil leaves. Drop the leaves in the water. Hold your hands over the water and mentally charge it with very bright, sparkly-green light.

Finally, drop a clean rag in the water and with the clear intention to invite in abundant blessings and opportunity, use the rag to wash the door.

Tess Whitehurst

June 27
Wednesday

2nd ♎

Color of the day: Yellow
Incense of the day: Lilac

Stand Your Ground

This is the feast day of Jupiter Stator, a specific aspect of Jupiter who aids warriors in holding their ground in the face of impossible odds. Are the odds are against you? Then, today is your day! In Rome warriors wore red cloaks, so put on some red, go outside and pick up a rock. Visualize the situation that has you overwhelmed. Fill the rock with all of your negative feelings regarding the situation. When you are finished, state the following:

> Jupiter Stator, a warrior
> I stand,
>
> The odds are against me,
> my fears in my hand,
>
> Like Romulus, I cast what's
> against me away
>
> Help me stand my ground and
> then win the day!

Let out a warrior howl, and chuck the stone as far away from you as you can. Then turn away and sit down. Meditate on Jupiter Stator's inspiration to help you to stand your ground.

Mickie Mueller

June 28
Thursday

2nd ♎
☽ v/c 4:22 am
☽ → ♏ 4:32 pm

Color of the day: Crimson
Incense of the day: Carnation

Increase Attractiveness Spell

Summer is in full swing and most of us are out and about in less clothing than usual—maybe even the dreaded bathing suit. If you have body-image issues, this can be a tough time. It can be hard to remember that what makes us attractive isn't the shape of our bodies or looking perfect—it is our spirits and our hearts. Goddesses come in all shapes and sizes, after all. The most attractive people are the ones who believe they are beautiful and project that out into the world—no matter what they look like. There is no magic to make you more attractive, but here is a simple spell to help you relax and feel more attractive:

> The gods they love me as I am,
> and so I love myself as well
>
> In beauty do I walk my walk, in
> beauty is the place I dwell

Deborah Blake

June 29
Friday

2nd ♏

Color of the day: Coral
Incense of the day: Mint

A Water Meditation

Please join me—It is nighttime and I am standing before a round pool of water. The Moon overhead is reflected in the water, and I can see the outlines of trees and bushes around me and around the water. There is a smell of pine in the air. There is a light breeze, and the air is slightly cool, but not cold. I look down at the water and step into it. The bottom is sandy, and as I take another step, my feet sink very slightly into the soft sand. I step in further and further, until I am up to my waist; then, I allow myself to float. The water is neither warm nor cool, and I am very buoyant. The water cradles me gently. I relax, close my eyes, and feel very peaceful floating in the water. I remain for as long as I need.

Magenta

June 30
Saturday

2nd ♏
☽ v/c 3:46 pm
☽ → ♐ 6:04 pm

Color of the day: Blue
Incense of the day: Sage

Meteor Day

Today is Meteor Day. This holiday commemorates the famous Tunguska event of June 30, 1908, when a meteor exploded over Siberia, flattening a large area of forest. A number of people reported seeing a huge fireball in the sky, followed by loud explosions and a plume of smoke. A traditional way to observe this holiday is to go outdoors at night and watch for meteors (though the best show is in late summer, when the Perseid meteors begin to appear in mid-July and peak August 9–14). Astrologers vary in their interpretation of a meteor's mystical energy and effects. Some believe that meteors, and especially meteor showers, indicate a brief but large boost in energy. Others say that a meteor represents a sudden discovery or flash of insight. So if you see one, be prepared to take advantage of the opportunity quickly, because it won't last long.

Elizabeth Barrette

July

July is the hope of April, the lushness of May, and the growth of June all brought to fulfillment. Now, flower beds are splashed with color, garden-fresh produce appears at roadside stands, and the Grain Goddess watches over ripening crops. The mornings are dewy, and there's a sweetness in the air. On July 4th, we pause to remember a special July morning years ago in Philadelphia, when statesmen gathered to declare that a young, struggling nation was free and independent. In colonial times, the Full Moon of July was called the Blessing Moon. Independence Day is the main holiday of the month, celebrated with parades and barbecues. It's also a good day to declare magical goals to free ourselves from bad habits and patterns. With the Sun in the water sign Cancer, cleansing and fertility magic of all kinds are appropriate. Simply taking a swim will cleanse your body, mind, and spirit. More than anything, July dazzles us. July is an awesome thunderstorm on a hot afternoon. It's a meadow turned white with Queen Anne's lace, and it's firefly nights. July is summer's song being sung. Sweet July—it's the high note of the year.

James Kambos

July 1
Sunday

2nd ♐

Color of the day: Amber
Incense of the day: Almond

A Rosemary Infusion for Your Workspace

Rosemary is a versatile herb that can be used to help you focus on tasks at hand, calm your mind, and add a bit of clarity to any situation that requires precision. Because the herb is a purifier, you can create an infusion to bless your office, study, or workspace. First, make a strong tea of rosemary. Take three sips and say into the cup:

Rosemary, purifier;
Rosemary, invigorator;
Rosemary, knowledge-bringer
—clear this space,
focus this mind,
and bless this work.
So mote it be.

Carefully asperge the contents in your workspace, getting the infusion on the desk, floor, walls, and surrounding space (but don't drench any electronics or paperwork!). Finish by setting the wet rosemary herb (used to make the tea) on a paper towel to dry. Once it's dry, put the herb in a sachet bag and keep it in a workspace desk drawer.

Raven Digitalis

July 2
Monday

2nd ♐
☽ v/c 6:21 pm
☽ → ♑ 6:51 pm

Color of the day: White
Incense of the day: Narcissus

Lead: Protections and Defense

Dense and heavy, lead was known to the ancients as a "poor metal." Never considered precious by alchemists, they nonetheless sought to change it into gold. Medieval pilgrims wore lead badges to symbolize their heavy hearts. Lead is dangerously toxic in its pure state, and many Renaissance painters are known to have been poisoned by lead-based oils.

In magical terms, lead corresponds with the Earth element and the planet Saturn. While its density and heft make it a symbol of endurance and fortitude, its energy is receptive and useful for divination, protection, and defense. Small lead fishing weights are handy for spell work. Use lead to manifest a psychic shield against unsafe energies, or use its weight to show burden, misfortune, or bad luck. Its malleability can allude to receptivity, or the ability to change. Lead symbolizes the characteristics *In Terra veritas*: In the Earth, truth.

Susan Pesznecker

July 3
Tuesday

2nd ♑

Full Moon 2:52 pm

Color of the day: Maroon
Incense of the day: Ginger

Larkspur Full Moon Spell

The larkspur, also known as the delphinium, is sacred to Venus, as are most blue flowers. It is often used in flower fascinations for love and protection. This flower can be readily found at the florist if you have trouble growing it in your own gardens.

Here is a Full Moon spell for you. Slip three gorgeous stalks of blue delphinium into a water-filled vase and enjoy their scent and their magic. Light three white candles for the three faces of the Goddess, and say:

Larkspur, by your magic a loving spell I do now weave,

Under the Full Moon tonight and by the power of three.

May I be surrounded by the joy and strength of love,

While the Lady shines down her blessings from up above.

May I know your blessings and accept your lessons true,

Guide and watch over my magic in all that I do.

Allow the candles to burn out in a safe place. Permit the flowers to fade. The magic will continue as long as your flowers hold. Then return the spent flowers neatly to nature.

Ellen Dugan

NOTES:

July 4
Wednesday

Independence Day

 3rd ♑
))) v/c 8:25 am

))) → ♒ 8:26 pm

Color of the day: Yellow
Incense of the day: Honeysuckle

Creative Energies Meditation

On a day when we celebrate our independent nation, we also celebrate the independent individual and revel in our artistic and creative energies. These can manifest in so many ways; you need not be an artist or designer to be artistic or creative.

Business ideas demand creative thought. Even the organizing of numbers by an accountant is artistic in nature, as long as they comply with accepted bookkeeping practices. A little examination of our abilities will reveal we are creative and artistic—as parents, as lovers, as workers, as healers, in our magic, and in the mundane.

We have become the people we are today because of our ability to see things in a manner that creates and re-creates who we are. We are a work of art to ourselves and others. Celebrate the independence of individual spirit.

Boudica

July 5
Thursday

3rd ♒

Color of the day: Turquoise
Incense of the day: Mulberry

An Ocean Meditation

Now that the Sun is in Cancer, it's a good time to take a trip to the shore. While there, you can perform this meditation. On a secluded beach, sit silently—watch and listen to the ocean. See the waves building, crashing, fading, and then being drawn back into the sea. Hear the waves as they crest, then subside. Now, think of an issue you're dealing with; see it as a physical shape on the shoreline. Watch as the surf washes over it; see it being cleansed by the tide. Each time a wave breaks, visualize your issue getting smaller, until it's gone. Return to your regular state of mind. Inhale the salt air and pick up an amulet from the beach. It could be a pebble or shell. Take this token home, and hold it if your issue arises again. As you hold it, see yourself at the shore, and repeat this meditation.

James Kambos

July 6
Friday

3rd ≈
☽ v/c 11:49 am

Color of the day: Violet
Incense of the day: Rose

Unconditional Love and Compassion Spell

Today is the fourteenth Dalai Lama's birthday, and here is a meditation of unconditional love and compassion for yourself and others. It's the White Tara Long-life Meditation. You can burn a pink or white candle anointed with sandalwood oil; and burn incense made of rose, sandalwood, and jasmine.

Get in a comfortable position and imagine White Tara sitting in lotus position behind you, facing the same direction. See the white rays of long life and compassion pouring out of her, through you, and from you to your family, friends, acquaintances, and throughout all humanity and life forms. If you have a rosary or prayer beads, you can count the times you repeat the long-life mantra:

Om Tare Tuttare Ture
Mama Ayuh Punya Jñana
Pustim Kuru Svaha.

Try to repeat the mantra 100 times or more as you visualize her white rays permeating all life.

Kelly Proudfoot

July 7
Saturday

3rd ≈
☽ → ♓ 12:29 am

Color of the day: Gray
Incense of the day: Ivy

Love at First Sight Magic

Tanabata is the traditional Japanese celebration of love at first sight, practiced in a culture where arranged marriages were once the norm. Doomed to partake in a forced marriage, Princess Shokujo fell in love with Kengyo. The Sky King forbade their love, but later allowed them to meet once a year on the seventh day of the seventh month. Tonight, practice Love at First Sight magic. Meditate on a person, place, thing, or idea that you fell in love with at first sight. Conjure the feeling, know the excitement of instant love. Place both hands over your heart and breathe deeply, letting love fill you. Then, exhale and fling your arms open wide, sending the energy out into the world. Know that love at first sight exists and persists. Keep it alive by cultivating the transformational energy within, and releasing it to work its own deep and abiding love-at-first-sight magic.

Dallas Jennifer Cobb

July 8
Sunday

3rd ♓

☽ v/c 7:00 am

Color of the day: Orange
Incense of the day: Eucalyptus

Crafting Magical Tools

Midsummer is an excellent time to craft your own tools. Finding things while you hike in the woods or stroll along a beach always feels satisfying and creates a personal connection with a wand or an altar piece.

Take your time, and look around while you are out and about. One of my favorite wands was made from three thin willow tree branches that I gathered right after a storm. Braiding the strands and allowing them to dry for a Full Moon cycle made for an excellent ritual wand. I've been using it for over ten years!

Paniteowl

July 9
Monday

▽

3rd ♓

☽ → ♈ 8:14 am

Color of the day: Gray
Incense of the day: Clary Sage

Courage

The world can be a frightening place, and many of us face challenges in our everyday lives that test our resolve and call for more courage than we feel we have. Tap into the energy of the summer Sun to recharge your soul's batteries and fire up your courage. Find a private place outside where you can sit under a tree. If you don't have a yard or a nearby wood, try going to a local park when it is quiet. Put your back against the tree and feel the strength of nature. Feel the warmth and power of the Sun. Draw these things inside you and know that you, too, are a part of nature and filled with quiet strength. Say to yourself:

> I am the tree,
> I am the Sun,
> I am goddess (god).

Repeat it until you really feel it!

Deborah Blake

July 10
Tuesday

3rd ♈

4th Quarter 9:48 pm

Color of the day: Red
Incense of the day: Cinnamon

Tefnut, Goddess of Water

In Egyptian tradition, Tefnut is
the goddess of water. She rules
over rain, dew, damp air, and other
forms of moisture. She is the sister
and consort of Shu, the Air god;
and the mother of Geb and Nut.
Tefnut appears as a woman with the
head of a lioness bearing pointed
ears (which distinguishes her from
Sekhmet, whose ears are round). She
was worshipped most in Heliopolis
and Leontopolis. People sought her
blessings for purification, health, and
water. Call upon her with this invocation.

Tefnut, sharp-eared goddess,

*Wash our hands with
pure water.*

*Sprinkle our fields with
clear dew.*

*Wrap our pathway in
silver mist.*

*From you flow the waters
of the Earth,*

*And to you all waters
must return.*

*Give us your blessing,
and grant us Permission to
borrow them for a time.*

Elizabeth Barrette

History & Lore
for July

It's the time of year to be especially alert for the sound of small whispers and giggles when you pass by gardens and natural places. It may be that a nature spirit—forest gnome, hobgoblin, or faerie—is watching you. Gnomes help take care of plant roots, and they have a strong intellect and intuition. They're also very sensitive to the changing energies of the Moon. Hobgoblins are related to brownies, and they are known to help not only around the house, but also in the fields at harvest time. They are fond of playing practical jokes on people, so if something is amiss, it could be that a hobgoblin is nearby. Faeries have a human appearance, and sometimes they can be quite naughty. They have been known to steal things—including children—and fly on stems of ragwort and the backs of birds, but they cannot lie.

Lee Obrien

July 11
Wednesday

4th ♈

☽ v/c 5:23 am
☽ → ♉ 7:30 pm

Color of the day: Topaz
Incense of the day: Lilac

Spell for Leftovers

No, not the kind that lurk in your fridge in plastic containers, but the odds and ends left over from spells and rituals. The candle stubs from a candle magic ritual that can't be burned the rest of the way. The money talisman you made three years ago, before you got your new job. The token from the Beltane ritual a couple of years ago. Anything that can be safely burned, should be; this includes candles, paper, wood, and natural cloth like cotton. The fire should be outdoors in a safe place, or in a fireplace. This does not have to be a ritual fire, but it shouldn't be a fire used for cooking either. Small ceramic or metal items can be buried. Small stones can be dropped in running water. Keeping these items blocks the flow of energy, so now is the time to let them go.

Magenta

July 12
Thursday

 4℞ ♉

Color of the day: Green
Incense of the day: Apricot

Solar Power!

We all need a little boost in the daily grind. If you're feeling particularly low on energy, go outside and focus on the elements around you. Feel the Earth beneath you, the air you smell and breathe, the water beneath the Earth and in your blood, and the fire of the Sun above you. Raise your arms and put your hands in a "cup" position, with the Sun centered in the middle. Close your eyes and feel its power radiating into your hands, through your arms, and into your body. Take deep breaths in through your nose and out through your mouth. While doing this, think of various solar deities (such as Sol, Helios, Ra, Pan, etc.), and feel the warm summer Sun pulse through your body and help carry you through the daily grind.

Raven Digitalis

July 13
Friday

 4℞ ♉
☽ v/c 3:46 pm

Color of the day: Pink
Incense of the day: Alder

Hieroglyphic Monad

This year Sir John Dee's July 13 birthday falls on Friday the 13th. John Dee was a famous occultist and astrologer to Queen Elizabeth I. There was a sigil he created and used to represent balance of the mind, body, spirit, and unity of the cosmos, the Hieroglyphic Monad. It's easy to find in any search engine and really easy to draw. Dee described the sigil as: "The Sun and the Moon of this Monad desire that the Elements in which the tenth proportion will flower, shall be separated, and this is done by the application of Fire."

It combines symbols for the Sun, the Moon, the cross, and the zodiacal sign of Aries. Draw the sigil on a small square of paper and carry it with you for good luck, happiness, and balance, and while you're at it, thank John Dee today on his birthday for coming up with it!

Mickie Mueller

July 14
Saturday

4th ☿

☽ → ♊ 8:26 am

Color of the day: Indigo
Incense of the day: Pine

A Sunrise Spell

Work this spell at sunrise and take a moment to embrace all the magic and possibilities of a brand-new day. There are no accessories needed for this spell. Just yourself and the sunrise.

Directions: Turn and face the east. Feel the warmth and power of the sun wash over you. Ground and center yourself, then when you are ready repeat the charm.

> As this new day begins, I
> stand and greet the dawn,
>
> May I help and heal others,
> and bring no one harm.
>
> I rejoice in the promise of a
> new magical day.
>
> Bring me love, success,
> and health in the best
> possible way.

Ellen Dugan

July 15
Sunday

4th ♊

Color of the day: Gold
Incense of the day: Almond

Land, Sea, and Sky Spell

The Druids observe and honor a pantheon of deities and the three realms of land, sea, and sky. Carry out a land-sea-sky ritual at the edge of a natural body of water: ocean, river, creek, or lake. Remove your shoes and stand barefooted on the Earth next to the water. Say:

> Gods and goddesses of land, pre-
> serve for me the here and now.

Step into the water and say:

> Gods and goddesses of water,
> preserve for me the mysteries of
> transformation.

Lift hands to the sky, palms up, and say:

> Gods and goddesses of sky, pre-
> serve for me the hidden realm
> and the shining ones.

Sweep your hands slowly all around you, repeating:

> Land, sea, and sky; Land, sea,
> and sky; Land, sea, and sky.

Before departing, make offerings to each realm: cornmeal or tobacco for the land, silver (a dime) for water, and dried strewn herbs for air.

Susan Pesznecker

NOTES:

July 16
Monday

4th ♊

☽ v/c 6:56 am
☽ → ♋ 8:31 pm

Color of the day: Ivory
Incense of the day: Neroli

A Spell for Abundance

The Virgin Mary was said to have appeared to monks at Mt. Carmel in Palestine on this day in 1251. This day is celebrated around the world in her honor. Since the Holy Virgin is the Christianized form of the Goddess, this is a good day to perform spells for abundance and prosperity. Cut a small bouquet of black-eyed Susans and place them in a clear glass vase or jar. Set the vase on a mirror in front of a window where the Sun's rays can shine upon them. Replace the flowers before they fade three times during the week.

Try to begin and end this ritual on a Monday. As you set the flowers on the mirror, "see" the Goddess blessing your home with abundance and prosperity. Visualize the mirror magnifying and reflecting good fortune throughout your home and your life.

James Kambos

July 17
Tuesday

 4ℏ ☽

Color of the day: Red
Incense of the day: Basil

happy Birthday to the Queen of heaven, Isis!

In ancient Egypt, this day was celebrated as "The Night of the Cradle" and was dedicated to both Isis and her mother, the sky-goddess Nut. Because Isis is honored as an all-powerful divinity, today might be thought of as a genuine "Christmas in July."

To celebrate her birthday, offer her your adoration, and align with her potent energy; go outside just before sunrise, face east, and light a stick of incense. As the sun rises, kneel and say:

Happy Birthday Isis!

I offer you this fragrant smoke

As a token of my gratitude

And a symbol of my love.

You are the light of the world,

The queen of all magic,

And beauty incarnate.

Today, with the morning Sun, you rise.

If you can, bow until your forehead touches the earth. Then, relax and observe the rising sun and the ascending smoke.

Tess Whitehurst

NOTES:

July 18
Wednesday

 4th ♋

Color of the day: Brown
Incense of the day: Marjoram

Questing for Freedom

In honor of Nelson Mandela's birthday today, take a moment to look at where you put your energy in life. Tap into your soul's commitment to the journey that brings freedom by finding a quiet time to sit in silence. You may wish to reflect upon the active contributions you are making to your own spiritual liberation, to the well-being of humankind, and to the good of the planet. Light a pure beeswax candle and concentrate on the flame, knowing that fire provides a gateway to realization of the ego's limiting effects. Open yourself to the flame and, keeping your eyes open too, offer up those things that impede your progress, drawing them up from the area of your solar plexus. When you have nothing left to surrender, gaze steadily at the flame and speak your intention clearly. To help it become real, visualize the flame turning into water and flowing down to earth. There, in the realm of the physical, the quest of your soul will be invited to manifest.

Chandra Alexandre

July 19
Thursday

 4th ♋
☽ v/c 12:24 am
New Moon 12:24 am
☽ → ♌ 6:13 am

Color of the day: Crimson
Incense of the day: Carnation

New Moon Meditation

The New Moon phase is a time for introspection and reflection. Meditation using a flower for focus is a good way to refresh yourself. For this meditation, choose a single flower that you like and place it in a vase on a table in front of you. Light a candle or some incense if you wish. Study every part of the flower—the lines in the petals, the veins in the leaves. Close your eyes and see the flower vividly in your mind. Imagine yourself diving deeply into the flower's center. Then, visualize yourself as a flower. Next, try to see back in time to the birth of this flower; imagine your own birth. See yourself being reborn and refreshed as you meditate. Use this chant:

Body, mind, and spirit here,
Help me to refresh and clear
All that seems to weigh me
down light and free, I am
unbound.

Ember Grant

July 20
Friday

 Ramadan begins
1st ♌

Color of the day: Coral
Incense of the day: Yarrow

Letting the Lion Shine

In astrology, the Sun represents masculine energy and outward expression of traits. Its influence shows clearly, just like the Sun in the sky. Your Sun sign thus describes the most obvious traits of your personality. The Sun also rules the sign of Leo, the lion. Leo manifests creativity and individuality. This sign expresses the ego through big, bold actions. Leos make good leaders or entertainers, anywhere they can let their talents shine. Associated colors include red, purple, and royal blue. The metal is gold and the stone sardonyx. When the Sun enters Leo, let your inner lion loose. Don't be afraid to talk about your skills, as long as you can back up your claims with performance. Spend some time on crafts, singing, and dancing, or other creative pursuits. Do something physical to use the intense solar energy. Look for leadership opportunities.

Elizabeth Barrette

July 21
Saturday

1st ♌
☽ v/c 1:17 am
☽ → ♍ 1:24 pm

Color of the day: Blue
Incense of the day: Ivy

Contemplation on Aten

The birthday of Egyptian God Aten is celebrated today. As the ancient Egyptian Sun god, he shares the heavens with Ra, Horus, and all the other Egyptian gods. He is the Disk of the Sun, with many rays, and honored as a creation god.

He was promoted by Amenhotep IV to the position of singular god of the Egyptians, to the exclusion of worship of all other gods. Amenhotep IV changed his name to Akhenaten to honor him. This was the introduction of monotheism to the Egyptian people, which was not well received. After the death of Akhenaten, the Egyptian people returned to their polytheistic practices. Amenhotep's successors were so hostile to his changes that they removed his name and reign from their texts. We are reminded here that we should not allow ourselves to become exclusive in our beliefs and practices, but inclusive of all gods, religions, and spiritualties.

Boudica

July 22
Sunday

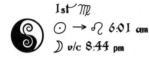

1st ♍

☉ → ♌ 6:01 am
☽ v/c 8:44 pm

Color of the day: Yellow
Incense of the day: Hyacinth

Tree and Fieldstone Rescue

If you're feeling overwhelmed or unpleasantly challenged in any way, find a natural setting with trees (if necessary, this can be your backyard). Walk slowly while taking deep breaths.

Now, become aware that there's one tree in particular that wants to help you. Follow your intuition as you continue to slowly walk. When you find your tree, approach it with reverence and respect (don't worry—you can't go the wrong way or pick the wrong tree). Touch the trunk and silently commune with the tree. Explain your troubles, and allow yourself to receive its healing energy and wise counsel.

When this feels complete, you realize that the tree wants to give you a gift. Allow yourself to be led to a rock. Pick it up and notice its grounding and therapeutic vibration. Thank the tree, and thank the rock. Keep the rock close whenever you need a little extra support.

Tess Whitehurst

July 23
Monday

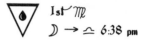

1st ♍

☽ → ♎ 6:38 pm

Color of the day: White
Incense of the day: Neroli

May They Never Thirst

The festival of Neptunalia began on this day, as did the Egyptian Dog Days. Celebrate by asking Neptune to ensure that all dogs, especially strays, have access to water. Anoint a blue candle with eucalyptus oil and consecrate it to both Anubis and Neptune. Light it and ask them both to assist you in a meditation on all dogs having access to water.

It might sound silly, but have a bowl of water ready and lap at it like a dog, imagining that all dogs around the world can find water. Feel the satisfaction of a dry thirst being quenched. Imagine dogs playfully romping near water, lapping, and enjoying its life-giving qualities.

Burn bladderwrack, althea, and fern, while you meditate on Anubis and Neptune working together to seek out all thirsty dogs, ensuring their safety and health. Be extra kind to the dogs you come across on this day.

Kelly Proudfoot

July 24
Tuesday

 1st ♎

Color of the day: Black
Incense of the day: Cinnamon

Fertility Spell

This is the birthday of Robert Graves, who wrote *The White Goddess*, the book that introduced many people, including modern Pagans, to the concept of the Maiden, Mother, and Crone, the Goddess of Birth, Love and Death, and the New, Full, and Old Moon. He is reputed to have written this fertility spell.

Cut an apple in half cross-wise to reveal the five-fold pattern, the pentagram, in the middle. Take five apple seeds out, and place them on your bed. When you put down the first seed, say:

"Aah," the second seed, "oh" (to rhyme with go), the third seed, "ou" (to rhyme with you), the fourth seed "aay" (to rhyme with say), the fifth seed, "eee" (to rhyme with be). Then, swallow the first seed, and put the rest in your garden, or on the ground in a park or other place where plants are growing.

Magenta

July 25
Wednesday

 1st ♎
☽ v/c 11:22 am
☽ → ♏ 10:29 pm

Color of the day: Yellow
Incense of the day: Bay laurel

Spell for Clearing and Cleansing

In ancient Rome, this day was known as Furrinalia, and celebrated Furrina, a goddess of springs, wells, and fresh water. So why not take this day to do some clearing and cleansing using water? If you can, go to a source of fresh water—a stream, pond, ocean, or river. If you can't, though, simply fill a bowl or basin with water. Stand in (or near) the water, splashing droplets over your head, or flicking them onto each of your chakras, starting at the crown and moving down. As you do this, visualize yourself being washed clean of any negativity or leftover crap. Say:

> Furrina, goddess of fresh water,
> wash me clear of all those
> things that no longer work for
> my benefit.

> So mote it be.

Deborah Blake

July 26
Thursday

1st ♏

2nd Quarter 4:56 am

☽ v/c 11:38 am

Color of the day: Purple
Incense of the day: Clove

Meditation to Release Negativity

Holding a grudge? Feeling betrayed? Now's the time to make amends, or let go. Start with a personal cleansing to wash away lingering residue from your emotional states and mental machinations. Draw yourself a bath and add calming herbs and essences. Reflect on whatever has gotten you worked up and resolve to find resolution, at least for yourself, so that you will no longer carry the weight of your troubles around. Relax in the water, slowly inhaling peacefulness and the lessons learned, exhaling negative feelings and thoughts. Visualize any bitterness, anger, resentment dissolving in the love of the Divine. Allow the stickiness of any leftover emotions to be washed away. Now, breathe in compassion and forgiveness, exhale ego. Repeat as often as necessary. Once out of the bath, take some of the water. On a day of the waxing Moon, pour a libation into the Earth to help strengthen your resolve to let it all go and find peace within.

Chandra Alexandre

July 27
Friday

2nd ♏

Color of the day: Violet
Incense of the day: Orchid

Finding Magical Tools

Summer is great for yard sales, auctions, and flea markets. I often go looking for something specific but love the surprises I've found while rummaging through other people's "stuff"! Like the small, black, not-very-attractive covered pot that is now a beautiful piece I display in my dining room. When I got it home, we sandblasted it and found the base is cast iron and the top is solid brass. Most people don't realize that I use it as my Cauldron of Care.

So often we hear about someone who is ill, or having a difficult emotional time, and we're asked to send energy. These requests seem to come in cycles, and in many instances, we never hear the outcome. When I receive the requests, I write the person's name on a slip of paper along with a one- or two-word description of their need. Into the Cauldron of Care they go, and each day I send energy through the cauldron. During the Full Moon, I light a fire in the Cauldron of Care, sending the wishes for healing into the Universe.

Paniteowl

July 28
Saturday

 2nd ♏

☽ → ♐ 1:18 am

Color of the day: Black
Incense of the day: Magnolia

Come Out to Play Spell

The Moon is growing, it's summer, and it's Saturday. It's a perfect day to cast away the trappings of your adult life, and let your inner child play a bit—you deserve it! Dig up one of your favorite childhood pictures and look at it. Remember that funny little person in the photo, and give them some love with this message:

> There you are my little friend,
>
> Been missing you a lot,
>
> Why not come out and play today
>
> And show me what you've got!

Now treat yourself to something you used to love to do as a kid, go to the zoo, do cannonballs at the pool, start a neighborhood game of baseball. Don't worry about looking silly, just do it—cast away your inhibitions. This experience will leave you feeling refreshed and renewed, and you'll feel less stressed for weeks. Maybe end the day chasing fireflies, but make sure to let them go.

Mickie Mueller

July 29
Sunday

 2nd ♐

☽ v/c 5:01 pm

Color of the day: Orange
Incense of the day: Heliotrope

St. Martha Anointing Oil

It's the feast day of St. Martha, who once singlehandedly slew a fearsome dragon. She's associated with magic of domination, and is suspected by some to have ancient, magical (non-Catholic) origins.

This oil is simple to make, and can be used to anoint candles, charms, and/or yourself anytime you'd like to experience victory or to be the reigning monarch of any situation. To make the oil, place a teaspoon of dried angelica root at the bottom of a jar. Add sunflower oil. Hold the jar in both hands and say:

> St. Martha I invoke your presence and request your aid.
>
> As you prevailed over the dragon,
>
> Help me prevail over everything,
>
> And dominate my realm.
>
> Thank you.

 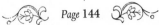

Feel the jar pulsating with St. Martha's potent power. Then, set it outdoors under the open sky until just after tomorrow's sunrise.

Tess Whitehurst

NOTES:

July 30
Monday

2nd ♐

☽ → ♑ 3:29 am

Color of the day: Silver
Incense of the day: Narcissus

Abundance

We are near the midpoint of summer. It's time to celebrate the abundance of warm weather, fruits, and vegetables, and life outdoors. Open yourself to abundance, knowing it flows freely around, and to each of us. Give thanks. Celebrate.

Invite friends for a potluck dinner. Ask each person to bring something they "love" to eat. As people, and dishes, gather around the table give thanks for your riches:

> The Earth is abundant, and the elements too. We give thanks for the warm Earth beneath our feet, the balmy summer air, the fiery Sun that freckles our shoulders and warm summer waters. Tonight we're blessed with friends, laughter, and kindred spirits. And we're blessed with food we love. The Goddess abundantly provides for us. Thanks be to the Great Goddess.

Dallas Jennifer Cobb

July 31
Tuesday

2nd ♑

☽ v/c 7:30 pm

Color of the day: Gray
Incense of the day: Cedar

A Spell to Protect Pets

Use this spell to empower your pet's leash, collar, pen, cage, and so forth, depending on what kind of pet(s) you have. We all want our pets to be safe, indoor or outside. We take all measures in the mundane world to keep them healthy and cared-for. A little magic can add to that. Chant these words as you visualize the item being charged with protective power:

> Where you roam
> or where you stay,
>
> Health and safety
> guard your way.
>
> You are loved like family,
>
> Be with me long,
> so mote it be.

Ember Grant

August

Named for Roman Emperor Augustus Caesar, August means "regal, dignified, or grand." It calls to mind the celebrations of late summer and golden fields of tall, nodding stalks of grain. It also begins the bounty of autumn. To draw the power of August into your spell casting, use its correspondences. Its herbs include angelica, bay, chamomile, fennel, marigold, St. John's Wort, and sunflower. Add grains, such as barley, corn, rye, or wheat. For stones, use carnelian or jasper. Burn heliotrope or frankincense. General colors are yellow, gold, and deep green. Most deities associated with August have a certain dignity. Diana, a goddess of woods and hunting, has a temple holiday on August 13. Thoth, god of writing and the Moon, oversees several feasts. Then there is Lugh, who lends his name to Lughnassadh and is a trickster and Jack-of-all-trades. Lugh celebrates this month with games and competitions. With those associations, what kind of spell craft can you work in August? Try rituals about gathering, harvesting, or preserving; and spells for health and vitality get a boost from the strong solar energy. On a more personal note, turn to appreciation and friendship—the natural counterpoint to the love and fertility focus of spring and summer.

Elizabeth Barrette

August I
Wednesday
Lammas

 2nd ♑

☽ → ♒ 5:56 am

☽ Full Moon 11:27 pm

Color of the day: White
Incense of the day: Lilac

First harvest

Today is Lammas/Lughnasadh (pronounced loo-na-sa), the first harvest and a day honoring Celtic Sun god Lugh. It's a time to be grateful for what you have and for your opportunities. In modern times, our harvests are often figurative rather than literal. Take some time to list all your accomplishments over the past year, and list your upcoming opportunities. Place the list in a cauldron or large bowl. Fill it with fresh fruit and vegetables and a loaf of bread. Then say:

> With the first harvest Lugh has filled my cauldron.
>
> I offer thanks for the year's good fortune
>
> My thanks for the harvest, the future to brighten,
>
> I ask for protection for my crops still to ripen.

Use the bounty of fruit, vegetables, and bread from the cauldron in your meals all week.

Mickie Mueller

NOTES:

August 2
Thursday

3rd ♒

Color of the day: Green
Incense of the day: Balsam

Protection Spell for the Children

As we start our preparations for the children returning to school, here is a small spell working to set up some safe practices with a little extra magical "push." I love the black stones you can purchase at hobby shops. It is not unusual for kids to have stones in their pockets either, because they almost always have "stuff" in their pockets.

Create a "protection" stone; a plain black stone anointed with a "protection" oil of your choice. I draw a pentacle on the stone in the oil with my finger and bless in moonlight. Give it to your child and call it a "remembering" stone. They can "remember" not to approach strangers near the school or while traveling to and from school, and they can "remember" to watch traffic when crossing the streets. Pick your favorite things your child needs to remember and give them the stone for their pocket to help them remember to be safe.

Boudica

August 3
Friday

3rd ♒
☽ v/c 3:24 am

☽ → ♓ 9:58 am

Color of the day: White
Incense of the day: Thyme

A Feast for Artemis and the Dryads

Find a peaceful setting, either in your own back yard or in a park, to hold a feast honoring Artemis and the Dryads (tree nymphs). If you have a favorite tree, set up under it or choose a tree based on the corresponding Dryad. For example: laurel for Daphnaie or oak for Hamadryads, and so forth.

Lay a pink cloth on your altar, table, or picnic blanket. Decorate with rosemary, rose, and acorns, or any flowers you feel are appropriate. Lay out a fine feast that you've prepared—maybe little cakes or cookies, a pretty salad, and some wine. Burn a white candle that has been anointed with sandalwood.

Give an offering of a garland made with some of your hair or ivy, strung with nine bay leaves. Bury it under your tree with a piece of moss agate. Give thanks to the Dryads for Artemis's protection and the beauty of the trees.

Kelly Proudfoot

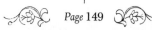

August 4
Saturday

3rd ♓

Color of the day: Blue
Incense of the day: Pine

Sunflower Spell

According to flower folklore, if you tuck a sunflower beneath your pillow, you can discover the truth in any matter. And working with the waning Moon will help to remove any indecision about your next move. I wouldn't have the heart to smash a pretty sunflower, but I would tuck a few stems in a sturdy vase and set it on my night stand. If you like, you could put a petal or two under your pillow. Try this spell just as you turn in for the night.

> Sunflower, tell me what it is I want to know,
>
> All doubts and indecision simply have to go.
>
> When the Sun rises in the morning, I'll know what to do.
>
> Grant me courage, confidence and the power to be true.

Ellen Dugan

August 5
Sunday

3rd ♓
☽ v/c 1:56 pm
☽ → ♈ 4:59 pm

Color of the day: Gold
Incense of the day: Juniper

Scholar Stones

As a graduate student, I assembled a set of stones to aid in studying and memory, and the results were fabulous! Gather your own "Scholar Stones" to help with your studies.

Carnelian: For self-confidence, inner strength, and the developing of insights

Citron: For mental clarity and supporting the transition between insight and knowledge

Fluorite: For psychic strengthening and connection to ancestors: a wellspring of strength and confidence

Jade: For wisdom

Quartz point: For guarding and replenishing energy and strength

Turquoise: For calm and tranquility and for ensuring health and well being

Hand-sew a pouch of yellow (for mental work and intellect) for the stones. Sewing by hand allows your own essence and energies to enter the work, and sewing on the waxing Moon supports ideas of strength and boundless energy and memory. Keep the stones near as you work; spill them into your hand occasionally, meditating on their strength.

Susan Pesznecker

NOTES:

August 6
Monday

3rd ♈

Color of the day: Ivory
Incense of the day: Lily

A Prayer for International Love

The world changed forever on this day in 1945 when the United States dropped the first atomic bomb on Hiroshima, Japan. The initial blast killed 75,000 people, and thousands more died later from radiation poisoning. And let's not forget that three days later, a second atomic bomb was dropped on the city of Nagasaki. This blast took the lives of 36,000 people, and thousands more were injured. Take time out of your day to think about, and meditate on, these tragedies. Our prayers and actions can prevent something like this from happening again. Find a quiet place and light one large white pillar candle. Let this represent every nation on earth, united as one great nation, brought together by love. Then, whisper these words written centuries ago by the great mystic Mevlana Rumi:

> The nation of love differs from all others,
>
> Lovers bear no allegiance to nation or sect.
>
> Now, go live these words and practice them every day.

James Kambos

August 7
Tuesday

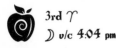

3rd ♈

☽ v/c 4:04 pm

Color of the day: Red
Incense of the day: Geranium

Spell for Relieving Stress

Most of us have to cope with stress from time to time, and summer seems to increase the pressure for many. We feel like we should be relaxing, and because we're not, that makes us feel even more stressed. Try this simple spell to help you deal with stress, now or at any time of the year. Fill a bowl with sand or salt (beach sand is great, if you can get it, but plain old salt will do). Light a white candle and place an empty bowl in front of you. Let the sand/salt trickle through your fingers into the empty bowl, and visualize your stress trickling away with it. As you do it, say:

I banish stress and let it go

Life's too fast, I let it slow

Calmer, balanced, happy now

To banish stress, this I vow

Throw the sand/salt away when you're done.

Deborah Blake

August 8
Wednesday

3rd ♈

☽ → ♉ 3:28 am

Color of the day: Brown
Incense of the day: Lavender

Automatic Writing

Automatic writing is a skill that takes practice, discernment, and discretion. Objectivity is undoubtedly a metaphysical person's best ally when discovering or attempting new skills. In other words, let's be objective with our results! To attempt automatic writing, get comfortable in a quiet environment. Use a pen and large pad of paper. Close your eyes and open your chakras. Then put yourself in a trancelike state. Let your pen write or draw whatever it wants; attempt to disallow your conscious mind from entering the channeling. Your mind should not be aware of anything the hand is writing. When finished, return to a normal waking consciousness, and use your objectivity to see if there are messages in the scribbles. Don't be discouraged if you can't make out even one word on the first attempt; this is normal. With enough time and regular practice, you may indeed find yourself tapping into external spiritual forces wishing to communicate by way of your pen.

Raven Digitalis

August 9
Thursday

3rd ♉
☽ v/c 2:55 pm
4th Quarter 2:55 pm

Color of the day: White
Incense of the day: Jasmine

Clothespin Spell

Are you in a deadlock over an issue with your boss, or do you have the same argument over and over with your spouse or a friend? Try this clothespin spell. Take two old-fashioned spring-clip clothespins. Name each, giving one your name and naming the other for the other person. You could even write names on them, or decorate them with something symbolic of the person. Clip the clothespins so that their jaws are interlocked. Spend a little time pulling on the clothespins, gently so that they don't actually come apart. Think about the conflicts involved between you and that person. Then, very deliberately, pull the clothespins apart, and toss them in opposite directions. Then, pick up the clothespins and put them together on your altar, facing the same direction, near each other but not touching. This should break the impasse.

Magenta

August 10
Friday

4th ♉
☽ → ♊ 4:11 pm

Color of the day: Rose
Incense of the day: Vanilla

heal a Broken heart

Loving fully means sometimes having a broken heart. Whether it's from a break-up, the death of a beloved family member or companion, or another type of loss—a broken heart smarts like nothing else. Time is the master healer; and when it comes to grief, there is no substitute for it. Making a habit of these practices can help clean and dress the wound so that it heals as rapidly as possible while you wait:

1. Drink at least half your body weight in ounces of water daily. Into each bottleful, add two drops each of honeysuckle and star of Bethlehem flower essences. Continue until the bottles are empty.

2. Spend ten minutes each morning and evening sitting quietly and noticing your breath. Notice the in breath and the out breath. When your mind wanders from the breath, just bring it back. If feelings come up, allow them and continue to breathe.

Tess Whitehurst

 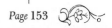

August 11
Saturday

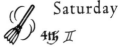 4th ♊

Color of the day: Blue
Incense of the day: Patchouli

Banish Fear

We all have a fear we'd like to conquer, be it large or small. To begin to overcome your fear, draw it, write it, or sketch a symbol of it. This is a burning ritual, so you'll need a safe container; this is best done outdoors. Consider this fear. Why do you have it? You may or may not know, but try to be honest. Imagine yourself in a situation but acting without the fear. As you visualize, burn the paper. See yourself as confident and brave. For example, if your fear is public speaking, imagine yourself in front of a large group of people giving a fantastic speech and you're completely calm and in control. Release the ashes of the paper to the wind—or bury them. Release your fear. Hold the positive image with you each time you feel the fear. As the paper burns, chant:

> Fire, take this fear of mine;
> I can conquer it this time.
> Learn to overcome alarm—
> Release me from this fear of
> harm.

Ember Grant

August 12
Sunday

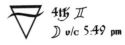 4th ♊
☽ v/c 5:49 pm

Color of the day: Orange
Incense of the day: Frankincense

"To Do" Today

As summer slides by, it's easy to be lulled into a sense of time-lessness. We can forget what we set out to do this season. Sunday, named for the Sun, is associated with ambition, achievement, determination, and inspiration, so it's a good day to revisit our goals. Harness the radiant Sun's energy to clarify intent, gathering the illumination and inspiration needed to accomplish what you desire. Lie in the Sun with your eyes closed. With brilliant light filtering through your eyelids, turn your focus within to see what needs to be done to fulfill your dreams. Renew your commitment to accomplish what you set out to do. Illuminated by the Sun, get up and write down what still needs doing. This is your to-do-today list. Get to work, and achieve a few small things. Affirm:

> I have the time, energy, money,
> and wisdom to accomplish all
> I desire.

Dallas Jennifer Cobb

August 13
Monday

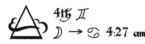

4th ♊
☽ → ♋ 4:27 am

Color of the day: Lavender
Incense of the day: Clary sage

Left-hander's Day

Today is Left-Hander's Day. Because of how the nervous system works, the left hemisphere of the brain controls the right side of the body, and vice versa. So left-handed people rely more on the right hemisphere of the brain. About 10 percent of the population is left-handed. In magic, the left side, or leftward motion, is association with receptivity and undoing. While most people project energy easier with their right hand and receive energy with their left, this is often reversed for lefties, who typically project energy with their dominant hand. They may also have a knack for magic that relies on some kind of reversal: banishing, hex-breaking, releasing a circle, etc. Try some energy manipulation today. Which is your dominant hand? Which hand feels more natural to use for projecting or receiving energy? Which hand do you use to hold your wand or athame?

Elizabeth Barrette

August 14
Tuesday

4th ♋

Color of the day: Scarlet
Incense of the day: Cinnamon

Poppy Spell

The poppy is sacred to the Greco-Roman goddess Demeter (Ceres), and I always associate this harvest goddess with this time of year. Here is a spell to ask for her blessing at this time. Arrange a few fresh poppies in a vase, light a golden candle for the goddess, and say:

> The poppy flower is sacred to
> Demeter and Ceres,
>
> Goddess of the harvest and the
> mother of Persephone,
>
> Bless me with wisdom and the
> richness of the earth,
>
> May I be surrounded by health,
> success and mirth.
>
> I banish all doubts and fears,
> by the waning Moon
>
> Great Lady bless my spell and
> please grant me a boon.

Allow the candle to burn out in a safe place. Permit the flowers to work their magic until they begin to fade. Then, neatly return them to nature.

Ellen Dugan

August 15
Wednesday

 4th ♋

☽ v/c 4:21 am

☽ → ♌ 2:05 pm

Color of the day: Topaz
Incense of the day: Marjoram

Travel Altar

This month is usually crammed with plans to travel, visit, or attend various events that may or may not be magical. Having your own portable altar can help you ground and center after a day of stressful experiences. The portable altar can be as elaborate or simple as you like. I've seen many hand-carved wooden boxes cleverly designed to hold equipment and also serve as a formal table for a working. I've also seen a small cosmetic bag used for essentials to create an altar in a few minutes! I have both, and I confess I use the cosmetic bag more often. A few white votive candles (keep it small and simple), a small jar of anointing oils, a small jar of sea salt, and a couple of feathers are all you really need to create a sacred space anywhere you go. Choosing the items can be really fun, and you can personalize your altar as much as you like.

Paniteowl

August 16
Thursday

 4th ♌

Color of the day: Green
Incense of the day: Myrrh

Divination for the Coming Year

Prepare a ritual bath with oil of myrrh and sandalwood and whilst bathing, meditate on the coming year and announce to the Universe that you wish to reveal what's coming for you over the next twelve months. Dry off and anoint yourself at the chakras with oil of frankincense, finishing at the crown.

Prepare your reading space with a purple candle consecrated with oil of jasmine to a deity of your choice, stating your purpose. Have a notebook and pen ready; burn mugwort, dragonsblood, and sandalwood. Occasionally, throw more incense on the coals during the reading.

Shuffle your cards. Lay out 12 cards in a clockwise circle, and place the 13th card in the middle to denote the general atmosphere of the year.

Interpret the first card for September 1, and so on. Read the middle card last. Record your impressions.

After you finish the reading, clean up and thank the deity.

Kelly Proudfoot

August 17
Friday

 4th ♌
New Moon 11:54 am

☽ v/c 1:55 pm

☽ → ♍ 8:33 pm

Color of the day: Pink
Incense of the day: Rose

The Key to Love Spell

This New Moon falls on an especially powerful day. Friday is Venus's day, a day to honor love and friendship. Also, in ancient Rome on this day the god Portunus was honored. His exact role among the deities worshiped by the Romans remains somewhat obscure. But, originally he ruled over doors, gates, and thresholds, and was depicted as carrying a key. So, if there was ever a day to cast a love spell to unlock the flow of romance coming into your life, this is it. You'll need an old key you no longer use. After dark, open your front door. As you stand at your threshold, hold the key over your heart and say:

With this key and the hand of fate,

I unlock every door and every gate

To let in the love which is coming to me.

With this key the power of love has been released

And is coming to me with speed and perfect ease.

At bedtime place the key with three white candy-coated almonds beneath your pillow. You should have a prophetic dream about your future lover. Afterward keep the key hidden, or keep it with other love charms.

James Kambos

NOTES:

August 18
Saturday

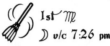

1st ♍
) v/c 7:26 pm

Color of the day: Black
Incense of the day: Sage

Simple New Broom Blessing

An everyday broom can be just as magical as a ritual broom (if they aren't one and the same). And the more we take our magic out of the circle and into the world, the more magical our lives become.

With this in mind, if it's about that time, lovingly release your old house broom and obtain a new one that you love. Place it outside on a clean white cloth, surround it with six quartz points (any type will do), all pointing inward. Let the new broom soak in the sunshine for 20 minutes. Flip it over and repeat. Then, hold the new broom in both hands so that it's not touching the ground, and say:

> New broom, new broom,
> blessed be.
>
> Aligned shall be our energy.
>
> Together we will clear the way
>
> For the bright and
> brand-new day.

Tess Whitehurst

August 19
Sunday

Ramadan ends

1st ♍

Color of the day: Yellow
Incense of the day: Marigold

The Samlesbury Witches

On this date in 1612, three women—Jane Southworth, Jennet Bierly and Ellen Bierly—were tried because of accusations of fourteen-year-old Grace Sowerbutts of practicing witchcraft in Samlesbury, England. It somewhat mirrors our own Salem witchcraft trials. But in this case, the women were acquitted. The women had been charged with child murder and cannibalism. The judge noticed some "goings on" in his cross-examination of Grace and her family, and it was discovered that the child had been prepped by her priest. Historians of this era suspect many of these trials were religious power plays within communities. The goal was to eradicate heresy, but many people were the victims of hatred and fear. Remember that not everyone was burned who was accused. But also remember what absolute power can do. Honor those who stood their ground. Remember those who suffered injustice.

Boudica

August 20
Monday

1st ♍

☽ → ♎ 12:45 am

Color of the day: Silver
Incense of the day: Narcissus

Make a God/Goddess Connection

The gods are always with us—not just from outside of us, but within us as well. But it is easy to lose track of that sense of divinity within. Use this spell to reconnect with your own personal goddess or god, or with deity in general. In a darkened room, light one white candle. Close your eyes and visualize a goddess/god. See their light, and see yourself glowing with light, inside and out. Feel the warmth of the gods reflecting inside you. Then look in a hand mirror (or inside your mind's eye) and see yourself shining with divine light. Say out loud

I am Goddess (God).

I am divine.

Repeat as many times as necessary

Deborah Blake

August 21
Tuesday

1st ♎

Color of the day: Gray
Incense of the day: Cedar

Gratitudes!

Every small thing and every precious moment offers a chance to express our gratitude to the Universe for life and living. Incarnation is a special thing, so take time today to stop and smell the flowers, sing your heart's praises, and give thanks to those who support you—from friends and family to the people who grow your food and do your bike repairs. And what about that Divine spirit inside that ignites your breath with a passionate response to the world? Be sure to kiss yourself in the mirror! If you want a delightful way to spread your love around, bring cookies into the office, send a handwritten letter to someone dear, and at the end of the day just before sleeping, speak the following: In gratitude for the gift of life, I send my prayers to all directions that gratefulness be found and hearts filled with happiness everywhere. Sleep well, knowing your prayers have been heard.

Chandra Alexandre

August 22
Wednesday

1st ♎

☽ v/c 3:13 am

☽ → ♏ 3:54 am

☉ → ♍ 1:07 pm

Color of the day: Brown
Incense of the day: Lilac

"Much in a Little"

Creating a portable, miniature altar leaves one ready to work magic anytime and anyplace. Begin with a small tin breath-mint box. Add a small stone (Earth), a birthday cake candle (Air and Fire), and a tiny shell (Water) to represent the four elements. A jar lid, or small spoon, becomes a chalice, while a toothpick serves as a wand. Cut a small piece of thin cloth for an altar cloth and include representations of deity figures. Small screw-top vials can hold salt, water, or oil with a tiny mirror or bit of glass providing a scrying surface. Add bits of herbs, a charcoal tablet, a few strike-anywhere matches, and any other items you choose. Store the kit in a purse, briefcase, or glove box, and you'll be prepared for magic 24/7. When you use it, incant *multum in parvo*: "much in a little," honoring your small workings as emblems of a larger result.

Susan Pesznecker

August 23
Thursday

1st ♏

☽ v/c 5:34 am

Color of the day: Turquoise
Incense of the day: Apricot

Prosperity Spell

Today is a good day for a prosperity spell, because Thursday is ruled by Jupiter, the planet most often associated with prosperity magic; and the Moon is waxing, contributing its growing energy; and because the Sun is frequently associated with gold and riches.

> *Earth, abundant, bless me,*
>
> *Air, breathe opportunity,*
>
> *Fire, passion grow in me,*
>
> *Water, flowing prosperity,*
>
> *Elemental riches surround me*
>
> *Bringing me prosperity*
>
> *Jupiter and Moon work together*
>
> *With the Sun's brilliant weather*
>
> *Wrap me in your riches.*

Dallas Jennifer Cobb

August 24
Friday

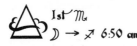 1st ♏

☽ → ♐ 6:50 am

2nd Quarter 9:54 am

Color of the day: Coral
Incense of the day: Mint

Fairy Bells

Good fairies bring joy and laughter to the world. They are associated with flowers, birds, butterflies, and other aspects of nature. Their magic helps keep the world alive and growing. These playful spirits enjoy music, wind chimes, and bells. Shiny things also catch their attention. One way to attract fairies is to hang small bells in your home or yard. String them on ribbons or wire hangers. Indoors you might want to put them near a window or fan, so they can catch an occasional breeze. As you hang each bell, say:

> Fairy bell so bright and clear,
>
> Bring the laughing fairies near.
>
> As they dance upon the air,
>
> Let them spread their magic there.

> When the bell begins to ring,
>
> May the fairies come and sing.
>
> Fairy magic, old and wise,
>
> Bless this place before my eyes.

Elizabeth Barrette

NOTES:

August 25
Saturday

2nd ♐

Color of the day: Brown
Incense of the day: Magnolia

Plan Rituals with Post-It Notes

If you are planning a ritual with other people, and you don't want to all be leaning over one computer, here's an idea. Get a pad of Post-It notes (or one pad for each person present). Use different colors and sizes if you wish. Write each component of the ritual on a different note. One note may read, "Call east," and the next one may say, "I summon stir and call thee forth," and so on. Put the notes on the inside of a file folder that you can close to protect the notes when you're done. You may need lots of notes to do this, but then you can rearrange what you are planning very easily. You can change which chant you use, who does what part of the ritual, or whether you invoke the God or the Goddess first just by moving around the notes.

Magenta

August 26
Sunday

2nd ♐

☽ v/c 2:39 am
☽ → ♑ 9:58 am

Color of the day: Gold
Incense of the day: Marigold

Ilmatar Invocation to Launch a Creative Project

Today belongs to Ilmatar, the great Finnish goddess of creation. If you're ready to officially declare and bless your commitment to a beloved project, call on Ilmatar. Even if the project is already underway, you can perform this invocation to lend divine orchestration to its completion and launch.

Choose or create a small representation of the project—a crystal, a statue, or simply write the project name attractively on paper.

Light a soy candle and a stick of pine incense. Say:

Ilmatar, Goddess of the Wind and Seas,

Creatrix of the Earth and all of existence,

I call on you.

Infuse this project with your heavenly help.

May every aspect of it perfectly unfold,

And bring waves of grace to the world.

Thank you.

Bathe the representation of the project in the candlelight and incense smoke, and place it on your altar or in a special place.

Tess Whitehurst

NOTES:

August 27
Monday
2nd ♑

Color of the day: Ivory
Incense of the day: Rosemary

Call Back Your Power

Sometimes in life, we lose bits of our personal power: traumatic events, destructive relationships, injury—many situations can cause us to loose personal power. But it's still yours; it's still out there in the Universe, and it belongs to you. So why not call it back to you. Lie flat on your back and close your eyes and visualize that you are under a grand tree in the sunlight. The tree represents the Universe. Talk to the tree, and tell it you have lost something that you wish to return. The tree rustles in the breeze and leaves begin to fall down, only a few at first, then more and more. As they fall, they seem to be glowing with life. As each leaf lands on you, it absorbs into your body and you welcome them. They are parts of yourself, your energy, and you welcome them home. Rise empowered.

Mickie Mueller

August 28
Tuesday

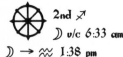

2nd ♐

☽ v/c 6:33 am

☽ → ♒ 1:38 pm

Color of the day: Red
Incense of the day: Ylang-ylang

Walking the Bounds

Walking your home's "bounds" is a powerful way to purify and protect that space. Circumnavigate your property three times, walking deosil (sun-wise) along the perimeter. On the first circuit, speak aloud to the house and grounds, reminding them of special or sacred times you have experienced there and offering your thanks for the protection and beneficence shown. As you walk, take note of anything in need of repair, and promise the house that you will make the needed repairs. On the second circuit, carry a lighted candle or smudge. Pass the candle or smudge over the ground, repeating, "I bless the bounds with energies of Air and Fire." On the third and final circuit, carry a cup of salt water and sprinkle it over the perimeter, repeating, "I bless the bounds with energies of Earth and Water." When finished, repeat these words of protection: *nil sine numini*: "Nothing without providence."

Susan Pesznecker

August 29
Wednesday

2nd ♒

Color of the day: Topaz
Incense of the day: Bay laurel

Self-Dedication

Feeling uncertain of where to turn in next metaphysical studies is common. This can lead to discouragement and even laziness. I know spiritual seekers who have felt either too inept or too uneducated to cultivate the self-motivation required in spiritual living, and who, instead, choose to depend on in-the-flesh teachers, priests, or priestesses to point the way. This mindset can be disempowering. If you feel uncertain, repeat this chant on a regular basis:

> *I am the magic; my spirit is the purpose; the wisdom of the world is at my fingertips at all times.*

Challenge yourself to spend time at the library, bookstore, or reliable online reference websites, and study concepts that have to do with religion, philosophy, human culture, and world history. Practice daily, and you will begin to discover your callings and will feel a greater sense of wisdom and personal empowerment.

Raven Digitalis

August 30
Thursday

2nd ≈

☽ v/c 1:48 pm

☽ → ♓ 6:31 pm

Color of the day: Purple
Incense of the day: Jasmine

Last hurrah of Summer Spell

Although we are constantly reminded of seasonal changes, sometimes we overlook the mundane changes that occur during the year. At the end of August, we should really acknowledge that an important change occurs when youngsters return to school. School buses affect our driving patterns, and events are scheduled around the school time-tables. In recent years, there have been atrocious happenings in schools throughout the country. We can all do our part to protect everyone's children by casting a spell for safety and success for all students.

- Use an embroidery hoop as a base (they come in all sizes).

- Stretch a piece of plan cotton fabric over the frame.

- Select a variety of miniature items to be used for the spell working.

- Hot-glue bay leaves and sprigs of rosemary around the frame.

- Stitch items to the cloth that reflect what you'd see in an average classroom, and please do include an apple for the teacher.

- Make a large hoop for your home and a small hoop for your car, and create your own specific wish for the health, happiness, and protection of our children.

Paniteowl

NOTES:

August 31
Friday

 2nd ♓

☽ Full Moon 9:58 am

Color of the day: Violet
Incense of the day: Rose

Full Moon Spell for Empowerment

This spell is intended to give you a boost of confidence and offer you strength in whatever area you need. It is especially useful if you feel emotionally trapped or insecure.

Dress yourself in black or white —a robe, if you have one, something that makes you feel powerful. Adorn yourself with any favorite pieces of jewelry you may have, or other accessories that give you strength. Prepare your altar with white and silver decorations. You can do this ritual inside or outside, but try to find a place where you can see the Moon, if possible.

Create your sacred space. Then, light five white candles in the center of your altar or table. Look at the Moon; feel the moonlight. Close your eyes and visualize the moonlight as a source of pure feminine power. Turn your hands palms up and imagine yourself catching the moonlight. Then, imagine it cascading over your head and shoulders, like water. Feel it flowing over your body, all the way down to your feet. As you visualize this, know that this soft light is strong and beautiful—as you are. If necessary, visualize yourself being free of a situation that is holding you back or see yourself gaining the strength you need to achieve a goal. Chant:

> Knowing now where I belong
>
> I am confident and strong.
>
> Meet the challenge, rise above,
>
> Achieving all that I dream of.
>
> I am strong and in control;
>
> I will reach my fondest goal.

Meditate for as long as you like, sitting near your altar. Allow the candles to burn out, if possible, and try to spend the rest of your day or evening relaxing and pampering yourself.

Ember Grant

September

September takes its name from the Latin prefix *sept*, meaning "seven," because until 153 BC, it was the seventh month of the then ten-month calendar. Even when the calendar changed, September kept its proud name. September is also known as Muin or Vine, the Celtic Tree month that goes from September 2 to 29. The magical associations of Vine month include fertility, prosperity, and binding. Just as vines can creep into everything, and bind onto outside structures, September is a month in which we creep into new environments and bind onto structures. Kids of all ages pack up and go back to school this month, back to structure and learning, tests, and scores. Parents shift gears too, imposing more structure on their kids, with earlier bedtimes and functional routines, plus falling into routines of their own: packing lunches, reviewing homework, and reading together. Like a vine in September, we hold on to new structures, climb toward new goals, and enjoy the fertile fruits of our labors. Take time to celebrate your accomplishments; identify what you have made, produced, or achieved over the summer; and vow to hold tightly to the structures that can support wild creativity. September is a time for all this.

Dallas Jennifer Cobb

September 1
Saturday

 3rd ♓
☽ v/c 4:02 pm

Color of the day: Gray
Incense of the day: Sandalwood

Cursing Spell

*The evil that you have
set upon me*

*I return to you,
three times three.*

Curse work has always been controversial in our community. Many oppose the concept of calling evil down upon another person, with good reason. The Law of Return can be a powerful reminder that we are not the self-appointed right hand of the Goddess. But cursing exists, and we should always be aware and be prepared to defend ourselves. We do not turn our cheek to have the other slapped; rather, we are warriors who will defend ourselves and our families and loved ones when the need arises. There is no shame in returning in kind what has been sent to us. A witch who cannot curse cannot cure. We cannot heal if we are always allowing ourselves to be hurt. Consider the use of the curse, but use it sparingly and wisely.

Boudica

September 2
Sunday

 3rd ♓
☽ → ♈ 1:37 am

Color of the day: Orange
Incense of the day: Eucalyptus

Cooking for Cernunnos

Celebrate the season by thanking Cernunnos for a bountiful harvest. Go blackberry picking (if you can), otherwise buy blackberries or other fruit. Make one of your favorite fruit recipes, or make a blackberry cordial, cobbler, pudding, jam, or pie.

Set up your kitchen as you would your altar, with a picture or statue of Cernunnos and a green candle that was anointed with patchouli oil. Set the candle in a ring of oak leaves and place a piece of aventurine in front of it. As you cook, think of the energies of Cernunnos—the protection of nature, the flow of the seasons, fertility, and so forth. Picture him in repose in the forest, with animals around him. Feel the energies of physical love, virility, and earthiness flowing through you. Drink a glass of red wine and toast Cernunnos. Pour a glass as libation on the ground outside your kitchen and leave a portion of your food as an offering.

Kelly Proudfoot

September 3
Monday
Labor Day

3rd ♈

Color of the day: Lavender
Incense of the day: Neroli

Labor Day

Labor Day is observed the first Monday in September. This became a federal holiday in 1894 to honor the labor and trade workforce. This holiday is traditionally celebrated with parades, speeches, and fireworks. Family barbecues are also popular. Today is an ideal time to cast a spell for finding a new job.

Place a newspaper on your altar. Roll a dollar bill lengthwise to form a wand. Point it to the four directions, saying:

East, south, west, and north—
a new job come forth!

Search the want ads and find at least one place to apply; tap the ad with your money wand, saying:

Energy of Labor Day, send a
good new job my way.

Release the circle. Unroll your money wand and carry that dollar bill in your wallet until you get a new job. Then give the dollar to charity.

Elizabeth Barrette

September 4
Tuesday

3rd ♈

☽ v/c 7:06 am

☽ → ♉ 11:41 am

Color of the day: Black
Incense of the day: Cinnamon

Guilty Pleasures

Sometimes, it's a good idea to do nothing for a little while. Today, the Moon is void of course all morning. It's a good time for those guilty pleasures—we all have them. Everyone needs time off from the usual schedule of work, school, housework, chores. As long as you don't break the law, your marriage vows, or a doctor's strict advice, indulge. Here are some of my favorites. Have a small amount—an ounce—of good liqueur, brandy, or sherry. Eat three scoops of excellent ice cream, scooped with a melon ball scoop to give doll-size portions, and served in an attractive little dish. If you usually exercise with other people, take a long walk by yourself. If you work out alone, make a walking date with friend. Read a trashy novel (my favorite is a Regency romance). Or just allow yourself to stare out the window and watch the clouds for a little while.

Magenta

September 5
Wednesday

 3rd ♉

☽ v/c 2:54 pm

Color of the day: Yellow
Incense of the day: Marjoram

Child Protection Spell

Many people find sending their kids back to school to be a scary time for both parents and children. Before you send them out into the world, do this protection spell (if you want, you can have the child do it with you—otherwise, use a picture). Anoint the picture or the child with a protective oil like sage, rosemary, or juniper and/or sprinkle with salt and water and smudge with a sage bundle. Visualize the child surrounded by a protective white light and say:

> Safe and protected, this child will be
>
> Until he (she) returns to me
>
> Goddess our mother, watch over my child
>
> With loving heart, both fierce and mild
>
> Keep him (her) safe from threat or harm
>
> With the power of this charm.

Deborah Blake

September 6
Thursday

 3rd ♉

Color of the day: Green
Incense of the day: Nutmeg

Morning Glory Spell

The gorgeous climbing morning glory is a protective flower. Its foliage, blossoms, and vines can all be worked into protection and binding spells and charms. As we have a waning Moon, let's conjure up a floral fascination-style binding spell.

Write the troublemaker's full name on a piece of paper. If you can obtain their signature, or a photo of only the person, then add that as well. Wrap morning glory vines around the paper so it is all bound up. Set the vine-wrapped paper down and focus your intention on the problem while you say:

> With this spell, bound hand and foot you surely will be,
>
> Unable to stir up any more troubles for me.
>
> You can break free from this spell, once you have learned your lesson,
>
> Be kind to me from now on, and all will be forgotten.

Ellen Dugan

 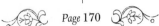

September 7
Friday

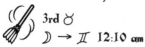

3rd ♉
☽ → ♊ 12:10 am

Color of the day: Pink
Incense of the day: Orchid

Conscious House Clearing

Salt absorbs negative psychic energy and clears space. This spell takes three days to complete, so start this morning, and your home will be cleared by Sunday night.

Pour salt into a glass or clay bowl. Sea salt or table salt will work, and a little works as well as a lot. Place the bowl at the hearth or heart of your home, which is usually the most used room of the house. Leave it for three days, then dispose of it safely. Throw the salt into a fire, a large body of water, or even down a drain with the faucet running. As the salt dissolves, so does the residual energy of fears, hurts, arguments, and sadness that your house has witnessed.

Keep a small bowl of salt at the heart of your home, emptying it every few days to keep your house clear. Use this ritual seasonally and practice conscious-house clearing.

Dallas Jennifer Cobb

September 8
Saturday

3rd ♊
4th Quarter 9:15 am

Color of the day: Blue
Incense of the day: Pine

Release Fear

Acting on fear can lead you to make some pretty serious mistakes, so release those fears, and they will have no power over you. You'll need a cord made of natural material like cotton. Build a small fire in an outdoor fireplace or grill. Take the cord in both hands and think of what your fears are. Begin to state them aloud, and tie a knot in the cord for each fear. When you finish, say aloud:

> These are my fears, I know that
> they are not helping me. I no
> longer hold these fears. I have
> faced them and I rise above
> them for they do not serve my
> higher purpose.

Toss the cord into the fire along with a handful of dried rosemary and sage. When you have released your fears, you can make good choices and avoid knee jerk reactions. You will now act rationally with wisdom and balance.

Mickie Mueller

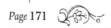

September 9
Sunday

 4th ♊
☽ v/c 6:59 am
☽ → ♋ 12:49 pm

Color of the day: Yellow
Incense of the day: Hyacinth

New Crayons, New Beginnings!

Remember the sweet, waxy smell of new crayons? Buy yourself a fresh box and use them to work magic for new beginnings. Select a new project, or one that needs completing. Choose a crayon color that is aligned magically: yellow for intellect, red for energy and power, green for success. Hold the crayon in your hands and visualize your desired result as you charge it with your vision and intent. On a small strip of paper, use the crayon to write out your goal. Grate a bit of wax from the crayon, and allow the gratings to fall onto an unlit candle; burn the candle and meditate on your goals until the colored wax is consumed. Roll up the paper and leave it on your altar. Carry the crayon with you as a talisman until your goal is achieved.

Susan Pesznecker

September 10
Monday

 4th ♋

Color of the day: Silver
Incense of the day: Clary sage

Fall Leaves Spell

It's always a good idea to use natural materials in spell working. Trying to incorporate exotic spices and materials can be fun, but our ancestors made do with the flora and fauna from their immediate environment, and so can we.

Gather a variety of leaves as their colors change. Press them in an album that has acid-free paper. After a week or two, examine the leaves and look for patterns, as though you were reading tea leaves. Each leaf will have its own story to tell you. Write your observations about the leaf on the album page. When you need material for a spell working, leaf through your leaf book. The leaves can be used whole, or they can be ground to make a powder.

Paniteowl

September 11
Tuesday

 4th ♋

☽ v/c 5:58 pm

☽ → ♌ 11:00 pm

Color of the day: Maroon
Incense of the day: Bayberry

Let Us Remember

We can all remember where we were and what we were doing on the morning of September 11, 2001, when we heard the tragic news that two airliners were used as weapons to destroy the Twin Towers in New York City, and when an airliner crashed into a Pennsylvania field, and another slammed into the Pentagon. Let us remember the heroes of that day—the passengers and crew aboard the planes, the thousands of people in the Twin Towers and in the Pentagon. Let us remember the police officers and firefighters, many of whom lost their lives protecting others. Let us remember the families and friends of the victims, whose lives were shattered in a matter of minutes. And, let us remember the brave ones who got involved in the clean-up and recovery process. Yes, let us remember and pray that something like this never happens again. Let there be tolerance and peace.

James Kambos

September 12
Wednesday

 4th ♌

Color of the day: Yellow
Incense of the day: Lilac

Repel Negativity Spell

According to flower folklore, the scent of burning aster foliage would repel evil. The aster is sacred to all of the Greek gods and goddesses. Since we are in a waning Moon phase, let's take this opportunity to get rid of bad vibes and stale energy.

Gather together some fresh aster flowers from your late-summer garden. Light a white candle and repeat the spell verse.

May these pretty blossoms help remove all negativity.

Dainty and fresh your magic packs a powerful punch,

For all your help little asters, I say, "Thanks a bunch!"

Allow the candle to burn out in a safe place. Permit the flowers to work their magic until they begin to fade. Then neatly return them to nature.

Ellen Dugan

September 13
Thursday

 4th ♌

Color of the day: Crimson
Incense of the day: Mulberry

Destroy a Curse Spell

If you feel you're the victim of a
curse, or just a run of bad luck,
try this old-time charm. You'll need
a large, rusty nail and a hammer. On
a moonless night, when the wind is
still and the clouds hang low, go to a
secluded area. Place the nail on a flat
rock and spit on the nail three times
with great force. Then, hit the nail
three times with the hammer. Each
time you swing the hammer say:

> With spit and nail,
>
> This curse is derailed!
>
> From here to eternity,
>
> Good fortune will favor me.

Bury the nail quickly. Return in
three days to retrieve the nail, then
hide the nail in an old rag. Repeat
this spell if necessary during a waning Moon. When good fortune
returns to you, bury the nail and rag
far from your home and never use it
again.

James Kambos

September 14
Friday

 4th ♌
D v/c 1:14 am
D → ♍ 5:30 am

Color of the day: Purple
Incense of the day: Cypress

Enchanting Food and Drink

We find ourselves in the thick
of the harvest season. As
part of your magic dealing with the
Earth's harvest, it's essential to bring
some extra thought into what you
consume. What is the origin of your
food? What is its carbon footprint?
Is it natural or synthetic, organic
or genetically modified? Before you
eat or drink anything, give a bit of
thanks to the earth and the harvest.
Look at your food and drink and contemplate its origins and various components. Holding your hands over
the food, close your eyes and silently
give thanks to the fallen God and
bountiful Goddess. Do the same with
whatever you are drinking. Conclude
by saying:

> I am grateful for the bounty
> before me, and send blessings to
> all beings who have helped pro-
> duce this harvest. Blessed be.

Raven Digitalis

September 15
Saturday

 ♄ ♍
New Moon 10:11 pm

Color of the day: Ivy
Incense of the day: Brown

New Moon Ritual

This New Moon is a good time to focus on new-money energy. Looking for a new job, a raise, or a new business venture? Here is a working to start. Focus your New Moon ritual on acquiring money or getting ahead on your bills. Start a new process for managing your budget or handling cash. Take an assessment of what you need in the next few months and see how you can work out payments for what you need. Replace a failing appliance that is needed and ask the Goddess, on this New Moon, to provide you with the finances you need to afford the replacement. And ask her to help you finish projects that you have had difficulty completing. Make it a goal to finish before the next New Moon. Remember to offer two silver candles, one for the old project and one for a new project.

Boudica

September 16
Sunday

 1st ♍
☽ v/c 7:26 am
☽ → ♎ 8:55 am

Color of the day: Gold
Incense of the day: Almond

Shape-Shift with the Morrighan

It's the New Moon phase, so contemplate your personal connection to the Dark Goddess. Consider the ways you express (or repress) the energies of revenge, darkness, and the negative side of your psyche. Think of the Goddess as Crone and how she presents herself to you.

Carry a piece of lapis lazuli and a black feather (preferably raven). Visualize the Morrighan shape-shifting into the raven and shadowing your steps. At night, by a body of fresh water—like a river, lake, or creek—burn a dark-blue candle that you've anointed with oil of myrrh and consecrated to the Morrighan. Meditate on the mysteries of the Dark Goddess. Come to an understanding of your darker side, and resolve to overcome any negativities and to use your power of darkness wisely, and only when all else fails. Remind yourself to shape-shift into the raven when you wish to emulate this wisdom.

Kelly Proudfoot

September 17
Monday

Rosh hashanah

1st ♎

Color of the day: White
Incense of the day: Lily

healing Nature, Birthing Life

Medieval prophet Hildegard von Bingen spoke of the greening power of creation—*viriditas*. Today, harness your connection to nature to restore vitality, health, and well-being. Should you wish to conceive a child, this day is also auspicious for laying the foundation for such a blessing. Begin with a call to Earth, visualizing the light of the Sun on the horizon as it kisses the ground. Dissolve this into an image of reflecting pools for Water, and this into dancing flames for Fire. Next, bring your sense of touch alive by imagining the feel of wind on your skin for Air, and finally, reach into space for Ether. Find a single point from among myriad colors on which you can focus. Now, reach beyond this into Source and bring forward your yearning. After a breath, return to the elements, and begin to draw the light of Ether down to Air and so on down to Earth. Realize you are manifesting your intention by re-enacting part of the creation process. Once complete, put your hands in prayer position at your heart and chant "OM" three times.

Chandra Alexandre

NOTES:

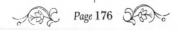

September 18
Tuesday

1st ♎

☽ v/c 7:30 am

☽ → ♏ 10:46 am

Color of the day: Red
Incense of the day: Basil

Scarf Spell for Protection

For this spell, any scarf or shawl will do. Choose one you already own that you like to wear or buy one that appeals to you—perhaps one that is decorated with magical symbols. Another option is to use a pin or brooch to accent a scarf and add magical symbolism. But a plain scarf will work just fine, too. Empower it so that when you wrap it around you, you can feel the protective energy. First, shake it out in sunlight and be sure that it's clean, removing any unwanted energy. Hold the scarf and chant:

Wrap around, scarf be bound.

By this spell, seal it well.

Safely guard, deflect harm.

Shelter me, let it be.

Visualize the scarf as a shield to deflect unwanted energy or to keep from attracting unwanted attention. You can also use this spell for a belt —just substitute the word.

Ember Grant

NOTES:

September 19
Wednesday

1st ♏

Color of the day: White
Incense of the day: Honeysuckle

Ganesh Chaturthi

The Festival of Ganesh dates back to early India. People celebrate it with performances of poetry, plays, music, and dances. Ganesh is the son of Shiva and Parvati. Usually portrayed as a boy with the head of an elephant, he brings wisdom, prosperity, and good fortune. He also has the ability to remove obstacles. At the end of the festival, he carries away the misfortunes of his devotees. In India, temporary statues of Ganesh are worshipped with elaborate ceremonies, then ritually disposed in rivers. Elsewhere it is more common to keep a permanent statue of brass or wood, and to use simpler offerings such as sandalwood incense. We can act in the spirit of the day, and say a prayer such as:

> Ganesh, lend me your wisdom
> that I may find good fortune
> by making the right decisions.

> At the close of your festival,
> take my misfortunes with you
> to your home in Kailash
> and scatter them on the winds.

Elizabeth Barrette

September 20
Thursday

1st ♏
☽ v/c 9:11 am
☽ → ♐ 12:34 pm

Color of the day: Purple
Incense of the day: Apricot

Athena's Smart-Money Spell

You'll need a jar, a picture of an owl, a bowl full of coins, and olive oil to do this spell. Look for a picture of an old Greek drachma. They have Athena's owl inscribed on them. Use a glue stick to stick the picture of the owl to the jar, and then carefully anoint the top edge of the jar with a few drops of olive oil. Place the bowl of coins and the jar near your front door. Every time you come in or leave, drop at least one coin into the jar and say:

> Lady Athena,
> your wisdom I borrow,

> I keep coins today, and keep
> them tomorrow.

Every time you consider a purchase, think of Athena's jar of coins and ask yourself, "Do I really need this?" By the time the holidays are here, if you are careful, you should have some extra funds for shopping!

Mickie Mueller

September 21
Friday

UN International Day of Peace

 1st ♐

Color of the day: Pink
Incense of the day: Vanilla

Peach-Ray Alchemy Visualization for World Peace

Alchemically speaking (and according to author Amber Wolfe), the energy of peace can be thought of as a peach-colored ray of light. Call upon and visualize this ray to bring peace to our hearts and to help shift the tide toward true and lasting peace in the world.

Relax, and slowly visualize your entire body transforming into bright white light. Then, visualize a brightly glowing peach (fruit) hovering about six inches away from your forehead. Smell the sweet aroma of this peach, and notice that its peach-colored light is blinding, like sunlight. This light represents peace, harmony, and love between all humans and nations. Now, send this glowing peach deep into the center of the Earth. See it expand to fill the Earth's core; then witness its light expanding and emanating outward until the entire planet is glowing brightly with the sweet and fragrant light of world peace.

Tess Whitehurst

September 22
Saturday

Mabon – Fall Equinox

 1st ♐

☉ → ♎ 10:49 am
☽ v/c 12:45 pm

☽ → ♑ 3:20 pm
2nd Quarter 3:41 pm

Color of the day: Indigo
Incense of the day: Patchouli

Balance

Today is Mabon, the second of three Pagan harvest festivals and one of two days in the year when the light and the dark are in balance. Also known as the Autumnal Equinox, Mabon is also the perfect time to do magic for balance. And which of us couldn't use more balance in our lives? For this simple spell, you will need:

- a black candle
- a white candle
- a pile of black and white beads, rocks, or beans

Jumble all the beads together, then sort them into two separate bowls, making sure you end up with equal amounts in each. Visualize your life in balance, and say:

Balance of Mabon, day divine,
balance in life, now be mine.

Deborah Blake

September 23
Sunday

2nd ♑

Color of the day: Amber
Incense of the day: Juniper

Amber Magic

Amber is fossilized pine-tree resin. It has the magical qualities of preserving the past, storing positive energy, and bringing about a balance of mind, body, and spirit. Amber is known for absorbing negativity and transmuting it into positive energy, absorbing physical and psychic energy. Associated with the third chakra, Amber helps us live our best lives and take action toward our goals. It can help us to overcome pain and move beyond a broken heart. Amber is considered to be a link between the earthly plane and a higher spiritual plane. Powerful for healing old emotional wounds, amber can work spiritually to simultaneously resolve old pain and shield you from negativity on a daily basis. Wear amber jewelry charged with powers to heal and protect by saying:

> *Sticky resin gather pain,*
> *Change it into power,*
>
> *Heal my spirit, make me whole,*
> *restore me to my power.*

Dallas Jennifer Cobb

September 24
Monday

2nd ♑
☽ v/c 5:19 pm

☽ → ♒ 7:32 pm

Color of the day: Hyssop
Incense of the day: Gray

Let Nothing Touch Me

Good spell work begins with personal preparation, and when casting protective spells, this is particularly important. Work at the Dark Moon and, if possible, when you have just finished your menses. Shower with frankincense soap (for blessing and purification); after rinsing, dip under the water three times, each time incanting, *noli me tangere* ("Let nothing touch me" or "Do not interfere"). Dry with a clean towel and don clean ritual garb or clothes. Light a black candle and place a piece of obsidian (for protection) in front of it. Sit quietly before the candle and stone as you ground and center. Cast a bubble shield, imagining a clear protective "shell" surrounding you two or three feet out from your body. Hold the shield in place as you once again repeat *noli me tangere*. Release the shield, extinguish the candle, and keep the stone with you as you emerge from the spell, protected.

Susan Pesznecker

September 25
Tuesday

2nd ≈

Color of the day: White
Incense of the day: Ginger

Ancestor Praises

We stand upon many shoulders. Take a moment to recognize that you are not who you are because of your efforts alone, but that you arise from the work, play, tears, and elation of many others. To honor those who have gone before and have contributed to your life and living, lay down five silver coins in a row. The first is for your foremothers, the second for your forefathers, the third for your teachers, the fourth for your guides, and the fifth for God/Goddess. Onto each one, place a pinch of incense, sugar, and salt, acknowledging the fragrances of living, the sweetness of successes, and the saltiness of tears spilt in both joy and upset. As you do so, speak a word or phrase that captures your relationship with these dear ones. When finished, place each offering into a vase with water, adding flowers to celebrate the blossoming that is you.

Chandra Alexandre

September 26
Wednesday

2nd ≈
☽ v/c 11:33 pm

Color of the day: Brown
Incense of the day: Lavender

Humor Spell

We can use humor spells to banish bad moods. Make a point of collecting jokes that you find especially funny. Write them on 3-by-5-inch cards, or in a small notebook. When you have had a bad day, when the outlook is bleak, go to a room where you usually practice magic, and cast a circle. Think about one thing that has gone wrong, or is going wrong, or that you are afraid will go wrong. Then read one joke out loud. Allow yourself to laugh as long as you wish. Repeat several times as necessary, but not more than nine times. If necessary, read several more jokes out loud without thinking about anything else. Then, end the circle and ground the energy. You can also use a recording of jokes (either make one yourself or get a recording of assorted jokes). The jokes, of course, all have to be hilarious to you personally.

Magenta

September 27
Thursday

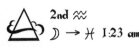

2nd ♒
☽ → ♓ 1:23 am

Color of the day: White
Incense of the day: Clove

Expand Your Horizons Spell

Today would be a good day to make a dream come true. Leaves are falling outside, revealing the blue, seemingly endless skies of autumn. And the cry of wild geese can be heard as they fly to far-off destinations. This spell taps into these seasonal energies so you can expand your own horizons by making a wish come true. Think of your wish as you follow this spell. When the sky seems to go on forever, and autumn leaves fall as gently as feathers, select a leaf colored gold or red. Grasp the leaf and envision your wish as these magical words are said:

> With my wish, I plant a
> magical seed,
>
> Here is my desire,
> here is my need.
>
> Just as geese fly, singing their
> haunting sound
>
> Let my wish be carried beyond
> the horizon's bounds.

Visualize your wish taking flight.

James Kambos

September 28
Friday
Yom Kippur

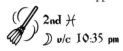

2nd ♓
☽ v/c 10:35 pm

Color of the day: Coral
Incense of the day: Mint

Apples and Oranges Spell

Fall is a colorful time of year. Use the colors and scents of apples and oranges to cleanse and protect your home during winter months, when doors and windows are closed tightly against winter weather. Use large oranges, or smaller tangerines. Stud them with whole cloves, and then wrap a ribbon around them and use the ribbon to hang them in your kitchen, dining room, living room, and bathroom. Peel and core apples, then roll them in cinnamon powder, lightly coating all the surfaces. Carve the apples to resemble a face. Set them in a dish on window sills throughout the house. As the apples "age," see if they resemble anyone you know. Perhaps an ancestor's face will appear. Ask the fruits to protect your home from illness, pests, and hardship.

Paniteowl

September 29
Saturday

2nd ♓

☽ → ♈ 9:14 am

Full Moon 11:19 pm

Color of the day: Black
Incense of the day: Patchouli

Egg-cently Banish Negativity

A time-honored practice for cleansing negativity, and for personal divination, makes use of a single egg. For this magic, you will want to acquire some all-natural, ethically produced, eco-friendly eggs. (Factory-farmed battery-cage eggs are latent with animal suffering.) Take an egg and rub it all over your body, or have a friend do this and switch off with a new egg. While rubbing the egg gently on your body, visualize the astral murk on your aura entering the egg, safely contained and removed from your body. When finished, crack the egg in a clear glass jar and gaze at the patterns. When scrying, pay attention to any significant or symbolic shapes that form in the yolk and white. Ask yourself how this pattern or image applies to your life and the energies you've just removed. Finally, pour the contents at the base of a tree and throw the eggshell behind your back to banish the negativity.

Raven Digitalis

September 30
Sunday

3rd ♈

Color of the day: Yellow
Incense of the day: Hyacinth

A Daily Blessing

Sundays are good days to connect with the power of the Sun and harness some positive energy in your life. You can also use this spell for the start of your work week, or any day you feel the need to boost your energy or evoke a positive attitude. Burn frankincense during this spell and, if you'd like, charge a piece of pyrite or tiger eye to carry with you. Hold the stone in your hand as you chant:

A new day dawns,

I'm glad to be

Alive and filled with energy.

I feel the sunlight filling me,

Bless me with serenity.

Ember Grant

NOTES:

October

"Halloweeeen, the witches riding high … Have you seeeen their shadows in the sky?" So begins a rhyme I learned as a grade school student. Halloween then was October's crown, a magical time of mystery and excitement—and a time to fill a pillowcase with candy bars in a hours-long orgy of trick-or-treating. The magic of Halloween and Samhain is still with me; my love for the month of October grows stronger with each passing year. October is all about preparation—and change. The weather dampens, temperatures drop, days shorten, leaves fall, and everything ebbs as Earth slips inexorably toward winter's deep sleep. But even as Earth's energies seem to chill and settle, there remains much to do. It's time for wintering-in: to dress warm and light a fire on the hearth. Time to brew pots of tea and sink deep into books and study. Time to launch plans that will blossom in the spring. Magical tools begun during autumn and finished during winter and early spring will be heavy with accumulated power and intention. Garb crafted during the dark season will be rich with protective magics, especially if you tell your stories to the material as you work. Divination studied throughout these months will tap deep into your psyche, leaving you with skills previously unimagined. Embrace the lessons of dark, wise October.

Susan Pesznecker

October 1
Monday

Sukkot begins

3rd ♈

☽ v/c 6:32 pm

☽ → ♉ 7:26 pm

Color of the day: White
Incense of the day: Clary sage

Precious Pumpkin Spell

Have you ever enchanted a pumpkin? Use this simple protection spell to install a guardian at your door. Procure a pumpkin—they should be out in the stores now—and place it near your front door, either inside or outside. Don't leave it on concrete, which will make it rot. You can place a board under the pumpkin to protect it. With a black permanent marker, draw a small pentagram on the bottom of the pumpkin. When the Moon rises, hold your pumpkin in your arms, and repeat the following:

Precious pumpkin,
watch over my home

Protecting from bane
all you behold,

By the power of this fruit
in the pale moonlight

Shield us from harm
both day and night.

Leave your enchanted pumpkin as a watchful guardian. You may carve it no more than one day before Halloween, and when you do, save some seeds for magic in the future.

Mickie Mueller

NOTES:

October 2
Tuesday

 3rd ♉

Color of the day: Scarlet
Incense of the day: Cedar

Rune Cookies

Runes are an ancient method of divination. Each rune's meaning may stand alone or interact with nearby runes. So you can throw the runes, lay them in a spread like tarot cards, or draw them singly. Here's a fun variation on drawing single runes. Bake a batch of 24 cookies, one for each rune. (If you have extra, just eat them!) Sugar-cookie recipes work well, though you can use any smooth cookie. Now, make some red icing. If you have a "ribbon" tip decorator bag, use it to apply stiff icing. Otherwise, you can thin the icing and paint a different rune symbol on the bottom of each cookie with a small brush. After the frosting dries, turn the cookies right-side up so nobody can see the runes. Pass around the platter for everybody to take a cookie. The cookie/rune you choose gives you your message for the day.

Elizabeth Barrette

October 3
Wednesday

 3rd ♉

Color of the day: White
Incense of the day: Lilac

Charisma Enhancement Oil

This oil will give you a charismatic edge for special occasions—especially when you want to charm everyone. Just be sure not to abuse your powers, because this is not a joke. First, cleanse a garnet with white-sage smoke. Then, hold it up near your mouth in your cupped hands (right over left) and whisper:

I am irresistible.

Place the garnet in a small jar and cover with jojoba oil. Add 6 drops each of jasmine and ylang-ylang essential oil, and 3 drops of patchouli. Slowly, in a clockwise direction, stir with your right finger as you say:

My face opens doors,
My smile opens hearts,
My voice opens minds.

Seal the jar. Anytime you'd like to "amp up" your charisma, lightly anoint your wrists, belly, and pubic bone before you dress.

Tess Whitehurst

 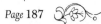

October 4
Thursday

3rd ♉
☽ v/c 3:44 am

☽ → ♊ 7:47 pm

Color of the day: Purple
Incense of the day: Clove

Meditation on Abundance

We often take what we have for granted, and it can be affirming to practice thankfulness. If you are reading this, it means you can read; there are many people in the world who cannot. Consider the number of living family members and the number of friends you have. Think about the cats and dogs in your life and realize that not everyone can afford to feed and care for pets. Do you have plants on your windowsill, or a garden? Those are living beings in your life as well. Look in your closet, and add up how many pieces of clothing you have—ignore whether they fit you, or are in style. Any clothing will cover you and keep you warm. Go to the supermarket and count the number of fruits and vegetables available to eat, and reflect on the number of places they come from so you can have a healthy and varied diet.

Magenta

October 5
Friday

3rd ♊
☽ v/c 5:08 pm

Color of the day: Pink
Incense of the day: Violet

Handle with Care Spell

Today, Saturn moves into Scorpio, which brings about intense emotions, secrecy, suspicion, and strong ego. While these energies can be beneficial when utilized for asserting yourself, developing your discriminating senses, and achieving success, it's important to remember to temper yourself with fairness, reason, and compassion. Remember to consider the pros and cons during this period. Mix together clove, cumin, and ginger for Scorpio; and cypress, poplar, and skullcap for Saturn. Place with a piece of carnelian in a red mojo bag. Anoint with sandalwood to soften the harder edges and carry it when you need courage or to enhance your personal power. To counteract the negative side of this cycle, make an incense of white rose, benzoin, and gardenia. Place with a piece of rose quartz in a white or pink mojo bag that was anointed with frankincense oil. Carry the bag to ensure that peace prevails.

Kelly Proudfoot

October 6
Saturday

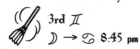 3rd ♊
☽ → ♋ 8:45 pm

Color of the day: Black
Incense of the day: Sage

Forgive and Forget Spell

How many times have you found yourself obsessing over the past, which cannot be changed? Cast this spell to forgive those who have hurt you and forget transgressions against you. Take back your worrisome energy and stop obsessing. Hold your hands over your heart and chant:

> *Like the Earth wise*
> *and knowing,*
> *I am always growing,*
>
> *Like the air that blows today,*
> *I let the past blow away,*
>
> *Like the fire burning bright,*
> *from what burns I make light,*
>
> *Like the water flowing fast,*
> *I move away from the past.*

Gently rub the area over your heart, and as you recount old hurts, feel them release from your heart into your hands. Now, forcefully open your arms and hands, casting your old hurts out into the world to grow, blow, burn, and flow away from you.

Dallas Jennifer Cobb

October 7
Sunday

 3rd ♋

Color of the day: Orange
Incense of the day: Hydrangea

A Ritual Cleansing Bath

Bathing is a sacred practice that many people take for granted. Many of us have the luxury of warm, running water, and, indeed, this is a blessing beyond measure. It's something people in many parts of the world would give anything for! To honor water, try taking a sacred bath. Create a mix of herbs and place them in a drawstring bag; you may wish to use cleansing herbs such as yarrow, sage, hyssop, rue, lavender, and so on (there are literally thousands of herbs specifically used for cleansing and purification). While you draw a bath, drop the bag in the tub as you would a giant cup of tea. Put four elemental candles around the tub and turn off the lights. You may also wish to put on relaxing music and light some incense. Meditate with the flames around you and intuitively summon the elements. While bathing, use all-natural soap and visualize your astral body purifying alongside your physical. Squeeze the herbs around you to release their energy, give yourself time to meditate, and enjoy the rest and relaxation!

Raven Digitalis

 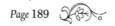

October 8
Monday

Columbus Day (observed)
Sukkot ends

 3rd ♋

☽ v/c 3:33 am

4th Quarter 3:33 am

Color of the day: Ivory
Incense of the day: Hyssop

Bedroom Spell for Restful Sleep

Begin by cleaning the space (a regular, practical cleaning); vacuum or sweep, dust all surfaces, make the bed with clean linens. Open any windows and allow negative energy to be dispelled. Then, burn sage in the room, and ring a bell nine times to purify the space. Light any number of candles you wish and assemble this talisman. Use a piece of white fabric and place moonstone, amethyst, quartz, and a small seashell inside. Sprinkle with dried rosemary, chamomile flowers, anise, lavender, and elderberries. Squeeze a drop of real aloe gel onto the mixture and add 3 drops of pure water. As you prepare, chant:

> Power of the silver Moon,
> allow your light to bless this
> room, to any here, bring restful
> sleep, safe and sound,
> this promise keep.

Wrap the bundle and place it under the mattress. Burn sandalwood incense and visualize peace and harmony in the room.

Ember Grant

NOTES:

October 9
Tuesday

 4th ♋
)) → ♌ 7:55 am

Color of the day: Red
Incense of the day: Ginger

The Price of Magic

The crisp air, sunny days, and cool nights give us pause to reflect during this very active season. Magic is, indeed, in the air. We need to consider what that means to us personally. It's good to know spells to help you improve your life as you go about your daily business; however, few stop to consider the cost of doing magic. Remember that magical workings are a form of energy manipulation and can have the same effect on you as when you stretch your muscles while exercising, or stretch your brain while thinking of solutions to problems. All can make you quite tired and, over time, deplete your energy. Consistently overdoing something may leave a permanent impairment. Using magic constantly, without developing your social skills, can harm you. Depending on magic to be your only talent will inevitably leave you lacking in other areas of your life. Make sure your studies and use of multiple talents will keep you well balanced and grounded. The key word here is balance.

Paniteowl

October 10
Wednesday

 4th ♌
)) v/c 5:40 pm

Color of the day: Topaz
Incense of the day: Honeysuckle

Demeter Blessing

In ancient Rome, this day was part of a three-day celebration of the goddess Demeter, called Thesmophoria. Demeter was worshipped as a goddess of the harvest and growing things and the mother of Persephone. At this time of year, it is fitting to ask Demeter for a blessing for home, family, and a bountiful harvest (whether it is literal or metaphorical). Assemble a bowl full of seasonal fruits and put them on your altar or a table outside. Light a white or silver candle and say

> With these fruits, I call upon
> the goddess Demeter to bring
> me a happy home, a healthy
> family, and a bountiful harvest
> of all those things I need.
> So mote it be.

Eat some of the fruit, and feel yourself taking in the goddess's blessings with every sweet bite. Don't forget to leave some fruit on your altar as an offering.

Deborah Blake

October 11
Thursday

4th ♌
☽ → ♍ 3:23 pm

Color of the day: Green
Incense of the day: Carnation

Cheery Calendula Spell

Calendulas are associated with the Sun and the element of Fire. According to the language of flowers, the calendula has the message of constancy, cheer, and hope. These flowers are easily grown in the garden or picked up at a local florist. Try a little flower fascination today and see what new positive things you can bring into your world. Gather together a little bouquet of calendulas and tie them with a pretty autumn-colored ribbon. Take them to work, or display them in a prominent place in your home, and cheer everyone up! Enchant the flowers with this verse:

> Calendulas bring affection
> and constancy,
>
> Weave your subtle floral magic
> all around me.
>
> Fresh autumn flowers do
> brighten up everyone's day,
>
> Work your magic for all in the
> best possible way.
>
> Blessed be.

October 12
Friday

4th ♍
☽ v/c 7:48 pm

Color of the day: Rose
Incense of the day: Yarrow

A House-Spirit Spell

> If you feel there's a ghost where
> you dwell
>
> May you find comfort with this
> spell.
>
> If you see mist at the top of the
> stairs
>
> Or there's a presence which
> moves the chairs,
>
> If there are shadows that float
> across the wall
>
> And you hear footsteps down
> the hall,
>
> When pictures fall from trusty
> nails
>
> Or if you should see a figure
> white and pale,
>
> If the lights flicker and go out
>
> And you hear things in the attic
> moving about,
>
> Take heart, do not fret, do not
> fear
>
> It's just a house spirit who
> wishes to be near.

Ellen Dugan

Welcome the spirit by placing a pair of shoes by the door and cleanse the space with a speck of salt upon the floor. When the clock strikes the witching hour, end this spell. Ply your guest with a sweet and a sip of wine, and wish them well.

    Peace—

James Kambos

NOTES:

History & Lore of the Opal

"Rainbow Serpent" is the name Australian Aborigines gave to opals. They told a story about the Creator who traveled on a rainbow road to spread the message of peace on Earth. As the Creator walked, the tiny stones under his feet and turned to opals.

In another story, when the Greek god Zeus defeated the Titans, he was so happy that he wept, and his tears turned into opals upon hitting the ground.

Archeological evidence indicates that opals were mined in North America 10,000 years ago and used for trade in Kenya at least 6,000 years ago.

Lee Obrien

October 13
Saturday

 4th ♎

☽ → ♑ 7:02 pm

Color of the day: Gray
Incense of the day: Pine

Dream Time

Midnight is the time of witches. Marking liminal space between night and morning, it provides opportunity for powerful magics and for potent dreams that teem with messages and import. Before going to bed, wash your hands and face and anoint your forehead with a dab of lavender essential oil. Then, slip into bed and incant the following acrostic spell three times, closing your eyes as you whisper the final few words.

> **W**onder where I'll be tonight,
>
> **I**n the silent land of nod.
>
> **T**aken there by heavy eyes
>
> **C**losed against the hours long.
>
> **H**ere the dreams come quick and wise,
>
> **I**nvented tales and mysteries spawned.
>
> **N**ight's denizens, their wits belied,
>
> **G**athering threads of stories long.

> **H**overing now, the dreams rely
>
> **O**n whispered shadows, fragile song.
>
> **U**ntil the cloak of night's disguise
>
> **R**enders light, the coming dawn.

When you wake the next morning, write down the details of your dreams and meditate on their meaning.

Susan Pesznecker

NOTES:

October 14

Sunday

4th ♎

Color of the day: Orange
Incense of the day: Almond

Welcome Winter, Bring Us Peace

Today is the first day of winter in some calendars, and it is a day to look ahead and make plans for achieving the fulfillment you seek. If you have snowfall, collect some for your altar to use in blessings and purifications on the way to inner and outer harmony. On a round piece of paper, write down the words that best describe what you need to do, what you need to clear away, and what you need to ask for support around in reaching your goals. Then, fold the paper in half twice and cut out a number of small shapes so that when you open the paper, you have your own snowflake. The words that remain untouched by scissors are the ones that will be your guideposts through the season for attainment of your desires. They will light the pathway to peace in your heart and soul.

Chandra Alexandre

NOTES:

October 15
Monday

 4th ♎
☽ v/c 8:02 am

New Moon 8:02 am
☽ → ♏ 8:06 pm

Color of the day: White
Incense of the day: Clary sage

Divination by MP3 player

Since many forms of divination rely on random chance, here's a twenty-first century method. Get your MP3 player, and choose songs for a new playlist. You could choose twenty-two songs to represent the major arcana of the tarot; or if you are really ambitious, seventy-eight for the whole deck. Or you could choose sixty-four for the hexagrams of the I Ching. Or just choose a range of songs that have some special meaning for you, and set up the playlist. Set your player on "shuffle." Think about the questions very clearly. It may help to say your question out loud a few times, or even write it down. Then, press play and see what song comes up. Listen to the entire song, paying attention to what it has to say to you. When it's over, stop the player, and think about what you have just heard. If you wish to use more than one song for a "reading" it may help to write down the titles, of the songs that have played, and imagine them laid out like a card layout or other reading display. Interpret the songs to obtain your answer.

Magenta

NOTES:

October 16
Tuesday

 1st ♏
☽ v/c 10:23 pm

Color of the day: Maroon
Incense of the day: Basil

Mojo Bag

Mojo bags—also called medicine bags, spirit bags, conjure bags, reticules, or gris-gris (gree-gree) bags—are wonderful for safeguarding runes, jewelry, tarot cards, or any magical materials. Any witch needs several of these! Choose fabric of a type, color, and pattern that corresponds with your desired use; velvet or silk are excellent choices for tarot bags, while washable cotton fabric is good with herbs, resins, etc. Cut a 6-inch circle for a small bag and a 10- to 12-inch circle for a larger one. Use a sharp scissors to cut a series of small holes around the outer edge of the circle. Thread a cord through the holes and tie the ends in a square knot, the knot's four "sides" alluding to elemental protection. Bless the bag under a waxing Moon. Cradle the bag in both hands and focus on protection while incanting *ad hoc* ("for this particular purpose") three times.

Susan Pesznecker

October 17
Wednesday

 1st ♏
☽ → ♐ 8:26 pm

Color of the day: Topaz
Incense of the day: Bay laurel

A Mission of Charity and Generosity

As this is the International Day for the Eradication of Poverty, enlist the assistance of Ma'at, the Egyptian goddess of justice, to help you in giving generously to those in need. Carry a red feather and a small picture of a heart with a piece of bloodstone and pray for Ma'at to lead you to someone who truly needs your help. Whether it be a financial donation, a bag of groceries, or a cooked meal, give it with love and don't expect anything in return. To start off the day, anoint an orange or red candle with cinnamon oil, and burn an incense of Job's tears or basil, cinnamon, and rosemary. Dedicate these to Ma'at and ask for her guidance through the day. Help out at a local soup kitchen or volunteer at a charity center. Whatever you do, do it with love and compassion, with no expectations or self-aggrandizement.

Kelly Proudfoot

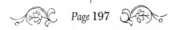

October 18
Thursday

 1st ♐

Color of the day: Turquoise
Incense of the day: Apricot

heart Strings

Meditate on your heart chakra. Associated with the color pink, it is the love center of our energy system. See the small tendrils of energy that stretch out from your heart, connected to the people, places, and things that you love. These are your heart strings. Examine these heart strings to see if any of them no longer serve you. Have you been draining energy into dead-end relationships? Have you pined away for an unrequited love? Do you give your love too freely? It's time to gather those heart strings. Envision yourself spooling them in, winding up the heart strings that drain your good energy. Use your arms to scoop them in, and your hands to return them back to your heart area. Like a spider spooling in filaments of web, gather your heart strings in, restoring your heart-chakra energy. As you do this, see the color pink intensifying and growing stronger.

Dallas Jennifer Cobb

October 19
Friday

 1st ♐
)) v/c 4:27 pm

)) → ♑ 9:41 pm

Color of the day: White
Incense of the day: Alder

Love Yourself

There's someone very special in your life. You see that person every day in the mirror, and you should remind them how special they are! Hey, you're a great person, and if you don't love yourself, how can you love others? Make a list of five things that you love about your mind, five things you love about your body, and five things you love about your spirit. Read over the list, then take some time to give thanks for being you and say the following:

> My guiding spirit
> I give thanks to thee
>
> For helping me to become me,
> For my spirit, body, and my mind,
>
> As I celebrate my being
> and let it shine.

Fold the list and place it with rose quartz tumbled stone or piece of rose quartz jewelry under your pillow when you go to sleep. When you carry or wear the stone, be reminded that you are one excellent person!

Mickie Mueller

NOTES:

ᛋ October 20
Saturday
1st ♑

Color of the day: Indigo
Incense of the day: Rue

A Spell for Time

We all have moments that we wish time would slow down. Either because we have a lot to do and not enough time to finish, or because we're enjoying a special moment and wish it could last. We all know that time often appears to move slowly or quickly, depending on our perspective. Use this spell to give yourself a sense of time moving slowly, allowing you to relax and finish what you need without worry, or to savor a great moment.

Hour glass and running sand,

Clock with face and moving hands,

Marking time upon the land,

Move slowly now at my command.

Ember Grant

October 21
Sunday

 1st ♑

☽ v/c 11:32 pm

2nd Quarter 11:32 pm

Color of the day: Yellow
Incense of the day: Marigold

Justice Spell

This is an opportune time to seek balance and justice, since we are still in the Libra zodiac period. There are often occasions when we feel that we've been shortchanged in life and wonder how to regain our balance. Using a traditional scale (one that has two platforms suspended from a fulcrum balanced bar), we can create a spell working for justice by simply placing items on each platform so that the scales balance evenly. For a specific result, select items that have to do with an injustice you feel you have received, such as a photo, a picture, or a piece of jewelry you've received from someone who has been less than generous with you. On the other side of the scale, place a list of reasons why you feel this is unfair. Make another list of the things you can do to right this wrong. Now, go back and make another list of reasons this person feels you have wronged them. Is your scale in balance? Continue to add things to each side until the scale is balanced. You really do have to consider both sides of an issue in order to figure out how to correct the problem. Once your scales are balanced, take the list of things you can do to correct the situation, and then do them!

Paniteowl

NOTES:

October 22
Monday

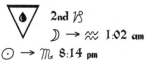

2nd ♑

☽ → ♒ 1:02 am

☉ → ♏ 8:14 pm

Color of the day: Lavender
Incense of the day: Neroli

Sun in Scorpio

The Sun is in Scorpio and we find emotional energies at play here that we may not be prepared for. Games are afoot, and sex and emotions are the victims or the prizes. As we move into Scorpio, be aware of the draw for emotional release. The house of Scorpio can play as well as give, and if we are not aware of which end we are on, we can end up with confused feelings and a broken heart. Be aware of your sexual and emotional needs. Allow time for both in your life, but remember that love is not a game. Nor is it a tool. Love should be freely given and freely received with no strings attached. If commitment is part of the package, give it seriously and stick to your word. Give love as you would receive it, in perfect trust!

Boudica

October 23
Tuesday

2nd ♒

☽ v/c 9:27 pm

Color of the day: Geranium
Incense of the day: Black

A Nutty Blessing

Two sacred trees in Druidic tradition are the hazel and the oak. The hazel is the tree of wisdom and associated with the arts of meditation and poetry. The fruit of this tree is the filbert, a favored food of dormice and gray squirrels. The oak is the tree of strength and is connected with the skills of endurance and leadership. The fruit of this tree is the acorn, an important food for pigs (both domestic and wild) and deer. For a Druidic blessing, gather equal amounts of filberts and acorns. Carefully pierce them and string them on a cord, alternating a filbert and an acorn throughout the string. Hang this in your sacred grove outdoors, or above your altar indoors, to bestow blessings of wisdom and strength.

Elizabeth Barrette

October 24
Wednesday

2nd ♒︎

☽ → ♓︎ 7:00 am

Color of the day: Yellow
Incense of the day: Lavender

Bring Nature Indoors

Many of us want to bring the natural world into our lives. That's one reason we share our homes with cats and dogs, fish and canaries. But some of us aren't in a situation to keep pets. House plants are a possibility, but what are other ways to bring nature indoors? In the fall, go on a nature walk and gather autumn leaves. Spray preservatives can be bought at craft stores, and you can pin leaves to Styrofoam forms in the shape of wreaths or other designs. You can go for a walk, and pick up rocks and stones, or shells if you are near an ocean, and arrange them in a bowl, or on a tray with sand underneath. Or get a fountain kit, even just an aquarium pump and a container, and make an arrangement of rocks and shells you've gathered, with water running over them.

Magenta

October 25
Thursday

2nd ♓︎

Color of the day: White
Incense of the day: Balsam

Divination and Synchronicity

The world we live in is alive and sacred. Many religious people tend to be unaware that God, or Spirit, permeates every piece of existence. Instead of projecting spiritual energies solely to outside forces, witches and magicians prefer to recognize the divine nature of all things. Because reality itself is spiritual on all levels, it is naturally communicating and interacting with us. As a result, answers to questions are around us and constantly taking the forms of intuition, synchronicities, and omens. Here's a fun magical experiment to practice through the day. Try asking a question of the Universe. This question should not be a yes or no question, but should, instead, be an issue or situation that you would like clarity and insight on, such as "What will happen if I take this job offer?" or "How will the party this weekend turn out?" Ask this question out loud, and continue mulling it over in your head throughout the day. Observe any potential signs or synchronicities throughout your waking day. Or you may, instead,

wish to try closing your eyes, thinking about the question, then immediately opening your eyes and looking around. Interpret any potentially meaningful symbolism, such as a stop sign, a newspaper with a significant headline, or even song lyrics on a random radio station. Open your mind to the ever-communicating Universe!

Raven Digitalis

NOTES:

October 26
Friday

2nd ♓
☽ v/c 11:04 am
☽ → ♈ 3:31 pm

Color of the day: Pink
Incense of the day: Orchid

Divination

As we approach Samhain, the veil between the worlds gets thinner, which makes this the perfect time for a bit of simple divination. Be sure to cast a protective circle first, though, to make sure nothing comes through that you don't want. Once you have your circle (which can be as easy as sprinkling salt around you and visualizing yourself protected by a shining white light), take an apple and start peeling it with either a peeler or a knife. (Be careful not to cut yourself!) Go slowly and carefully. Try to keep the peel in one long strip by going around in a circle from top to bottom. Let the peel fall free as you finish, and see if the shape it falls into suggests an answer to any question you might have. Cut the apple across and see the pentacle inside!

Deborah Blake

October 27
Saturday

 2nd ♈

☽ v/c 9:32 pm

Color of the day: Blue
Incense of the day: Magnolia

home Blessing Mist

This autumn-inspired mist potion will bless your home with sweetness, abundance, and joy. Wash an apple and hold it in your open palms to bathe it in sunlight for one minute. Place a large bowl in sunlight and fill it with water. Cut the apple into eight wedges and place them in the water. Leave for 30 to 40 minutes. Then, fill a mister bottle with water from the bowl. Add 2 drops each of the essential oils clove and cinnamon. (Be careful with the essential oils; both have been known to irritate.) Hold the bottle in both hands and visualize it swirling with sparkly, golden-orange light. Pour the remaining water around the base of a tree and dispose of the apple wedges similarly, or compost them.

To bless your home, lightly shake the liquid and then spray mist in each room and area, paying special attention to the front door and doormat.

Tess Whitehurst

October 28
Sunday

 2nd ♈

Color of the day: Gold
Incense of the day: Eucalyptus

Listening to the Other Side

The season of the ancient ones is upon us, a time of apperception, when we can come to new understandings based on our past experiences and learnings gleaned from our supporters on the other side. What do the spirits offer now? What are their insights? To find out, set up a scrying bowl or mirror. By the light of the Full Moon, delve into the blackness. Let the moonbeams dance and offer you wisdom about the past year. Pay particular attention to steps taken to no avail, to sufferings, and to letting go. Let truth emerge and take it in. Here, you will be ready for a revelation from something long considered over and done; there will be a gift in the darkness. Raise the question, "What do I need to know now?" and be open to the possibilities. As you reflect upon the meaning of the answer you receive, notice that a door is opening. No matter what you choose, remember to take the wisdom of your past efforts with you.

Chandra Alexandre

October 29
Monday

 2nd ♈
☽ → ♉ 2:15 am

Full Moon 3:49 pm
☽ v/c 5:01 pm
Color of the day: Gray
Incense of the day: Rosemary

Full Blood Moon Spell

Tonight is a perfect time to take a moment just for yourself and to celebrate your spirituality. As the full Blood Moon rises, arrange your altar as you like, with pumpkins, fall flowers, leaves, altar candles, etc. Then gaze upon those lit candles and take a moment to consider why you got involved in the Craft in the first place. Ground and center and remember the joy of the Samhain holiday. Now tap into all that energy that is out there and direct it into your life to help bolster up your confidence and strength of purpose. Look up at the Moon and when you feel its light shower down on you, and fill you with autumn's magic, say:

> As the full Blood Moon rises
> and Samhain looms closer still,
>
> I call for courage, determina-
> tion, and strength of will.
>
> During this dark time of year
> my magic lights the way,

> I call the Old Ones to bear wit-
> ness to what I say,
>
> Now gathering true wisdom
> and magic, closely around me,
>
> I am a Witch with power,
> compassion and integrity.
>
> By the power of the Full Moon
> this spell is spun,
>
> As I will so mote it be, An let it
> harm none

Ellen Dugan

NOTES:

October 30
Tuesday

3rd ♉

Color of the day: Red
Incense of the day: Ylang-ylang

Sunrise Spell

Work this spell at sunrise and take a moment to embrace all the magic and possibilities of a brand-new day. There are no accessories needed for this spell, just yourself and the sunrise. Directions: turn and face the east. Feel the warmth and power of the Sun wash over you. Ground and center yourself, then when you are ready repeat the charm.

> *As this new day begins, I stand and greet the dawn,*
>
> *May I help and heal others, and bring no one harm.*
>
> *I rejoice in the promise of a new magical day.*
>
> *Bring me love, success, and health in the best possible way.*

Ellen Dugan

October 31
Wednesday

 halloween – Samhain

3rd ♉

☽ → ♊ 2:40 pm

Color of the day: White
Incense of the day: Bay laurel

Samhain Fire Magic

On Samhain Eve in old Europe, the home fires were extinguished and great bonfires were lit in the countryside. The fires on cottage hearths would then be rekindled by embers from the village bonfires. This was done to symbolize that the fires would continue through the dark of winter. Fires were used to purify and destroy old habits, or anything negative, so everything would be cleansed in readiness for the new year. Fire was also used to light the way for the spirits that would be traveling during the night of this Great Sabbat. A remnant of this is still with us when we illuminate a jack-o'-lantern. To perform Fire magic at Samhain, light one orange and one black candle. The orange candle represents the last harvest. The black candle honors your ancestors. As the candles burn, meditate. Think about your connections to the past, and focus on the path you wish to follow during the coming year.

James Kambos

November

November may appear to be a brown and dreary month, depending on one's particular climate, but it holds a quiet beauty. While in our mundane lives we're often preoccupied with planning for the upcoming winter holidays, this time of year, as fall begins to fully embrace winter, offers opportunities to observe wildlife, star-gaze, and see aspects of nature that are sometimes overlooked. Observe the beauty of leafless trees; see their true form and shape. Look at fallen leaves, often etched with frost, and watch for trees bearing winter berries and cones. Walking through the woods in November can be eye-opening. Without the thick growth of underbrush, and biting insects, we can see a bareness of Earth seldom revealed. Work magic with the season's first snowfall, or save some snow for a future ritual. In addition, collect leaves, twigs, and nuts to make a wreath. Have a bonfire celebration; work Fire-magic. Think of November as a special time of waiting, an interlude between the vibrant fall and the coming winter. This is a time of darkening days, but also a time for indoor work or, if weather permits, outdoor magic. In some areas, this off-season is a great time to rent a cabin in the woods. Welcome the wonder of transition.

Ember Grant

November 1
Thursday

Day of the Dead
All Saints' Day

3rd ♊

Color of the day: White
Incense of the day: Myrrh

A Day for Remembering

Today is a time to remember those who have made a lasting impression on our lives. Yes, they can be Saints according to a religious belief, but they can also be those who have stood as examples, or mentors, to us in a variety of ways. Create an altar in your home that can hold a number of items to remind you of those people.

Pictures, pieces of jewelry, stones, flowers—all are appropriate for this type of "shrine." Plan a dinner that consists of comfort foods. Place portions of the food on a small plate and place it on the altar. Light the candles and think about the people you choose to include. Give thanks for their influence on your life, and send good wishes to those who are still in your life. Be assured they will benefit from your thoughts.

Paniteowl

November 2
Friday

3rd ♊
☽ v/c 5:21 am

Color of the day: Rose
Incense of the day: Basil

A Prayer for All Souls

The end of October and beginning of November host a cluster of related holidays honoring the dead and other incorporeal spirits. Many Pagan traditions feature occasions for honoring specific categories of the dead, such as family ancestors or fallen warriors, or those dedicated to a certain deity. Those not covered under specific categories, and those who were lost or forgotten, were often honored collectively. Christianity later applied this to souls not in a state of purity suitable for entering Heaven. Today, spare a thought for all the souls.

> O Universe that encompasses all that is,
>
> Let there be prayer for all souls today:
>
> To those gone missing in action, peace;
>
> To those who died of hunger, fulfillment;

To those who wandered lost,
rest;

To those who were forgotten,
remembrance;

To each what is needed, unto
the end of time,

And in the world's turning,
rebirth.

      Elizabeth Barrette

NOTES:

November 3
Saturday

 3rd ♊
   ☽ → ♋ 3:43 am

Color of the day: Brown
Incense of the day: Magnolia

What's Stopping You?

Sometimes a project gets away from us. We lose interest in what we really wanted to do. What is stopping us? Why can't we finish?

Road Opener Oil and a nine-day Road Opener candle are good meditative tools for looking for clarification on projects we just can't seem to get done.

Start with the candle and the oil. Anoint the candle and start it burning. Make sure it is on a surface that will not burn and where it will not be disturbed (accidently tipped over) but is clearly visible.

When you see the candle, take time to contemplate the unfinished project. Make some meditative time to understand what exactly is holding up your end of the project, and make notes. And be sure to consider what you need to finish the project, and how to complete it. Write it down and work on it. Finish what you start.

      Boudica

November 4
Sunday

Daylight Saving Time ends, 2 am

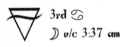 3rd ♋
☽ v/c 3:37 am

Color of the day: Amber
Incense of the day: Juniper

Reset Spell

What is there in your life that you would like to undo, turn around, rewind? This is the night for it: Daylight Savings Time is ending; time to turn the clock back. You don't have to stay up until 3 am for this spell, but perform it as late as possible in the evening. Find a old wind-up clock with hands, and a spool of thread, and think about one issue or problem you want to work on. Find a quiet place to sit with the clock, and have the thread within reach. Think about the situation you want to undo. Take the thread and unwind a few feet. Then set the clock back 15 minutes, unwind more thread, and set the clock back again, until you've set the clock back a full hour. Be sure to wind the clock so it continues running, and then burn the thread you've unwound.

Magenta

November 5
Monday

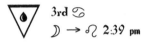 3rd ♋
☽ → ♌ 2:39 pm

Color of the day: Ivory
Incense of the day: Clary sage

Running Water Wash

Hoodoo and other magical systems believe that running water can purify one's energy while simultaneously washing dirt and dead skin cells from the physical frame. This magical principle makes sense, considering the flowing, rushing energy of running water. It is commonly believed that a person doesn't even necessarily have to immerse themselves in water that is in the process of running; in fact, gathering a bottle of river water or stream water can be sufficient because the flowing energy is inherently attached to the water. After having gathered a bottle of running water, add a few pinches of salt and shake up the bottle. Visualize the water glowing in purifying white and blue energy. The next morning (right before a morning shower), put yourself in a meditative state of mind and step naked into the shower. Pour the whole bottle over your head and, while it's rushing over your body,

 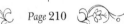

visualize it sweeping away stagnant energy while simultaneously waking up your mind for the day.

Raven Digitalis

NOTES:

November 6
Tuesday

Election Day (general)

 3rd ♌

4th Quarter 7:36 pm

Color of the day: Black
Incense of the day: Cedar

Doorway Spell

Before you leave the house today, do this quick spell to manifest a positive future. Carve the shape of a key onto a red candle and light it. Write down on a piece of paper the words:

> As I walk through the door I will see...

Then list at least five positive things that you want to see happen in the world. Read over the list aloud before the candle, and leave the list beneath the candle as you get ready for your day. Before you go through your front door, read the list one more time and blow out the candle, placing the list in your pocket. When you walk through your front door, utter:

> As I will it, so shall it be.

Go about your business of the day; when you return home, place your list under the candle again, relight it, and allow it to burn out.

Mickie Mueller

November 7
Wednesday

 4♄ ♌
☽ v/c 10:27 am
☽ → ♍ 11:35 pm

Color of the day: Amber
Incense of the day: Lilac

Nurture the home

As the dark increases, we tend to spend more time at home. Whether you live in a house or an apartment, or even a dorm room, now is a good time to do a little magic to nurture the place you call home. Start by cleaning up! Then sprinkle a bit of salt on all the doors and windows. Smudge with sage if you have it, and say the following as you walk around your space:

Home is where the heart is

And here my soul reside

Grant me warmth and safety

While I am inside

Deborah Blake

November 8
Thursday

 4♄ ♌

Color of the day: Purple
Incense of the day: Mulberry

Opening to the Underworld

With the journey into darkness deepening now, the question of how to sustain ourselves without falling into mental or emotional downward spirals comes alive. In part, the answer lies with drawing on a connection to the Underworld and the raw energies to be found there. Do you know that we can utilize the power of this realm to aid our well-being? First, strengthen yourself through regular breathing exercises such as pranayama. Opening to the Underworld takes strength and courage, resolve and will; cultivate these. Focus your intention on moving past extant hurdles or anticipated ones in your life and ask for a guide to come forward. As you are ready, draw up the energy offered by the lower worlds to help you stay healthy in mind, body, and spirit. Because such a gift requires an equal exchange, be sure to make a conscious sacrifice in the subtle realm before you are through.

Chandra Alexandre

November 9
Friday

 4th ♏
)) v/c 7:27 pm

Color of the day: Maroon
Incense of the day: Bayberry

Chrysanthemum Spell

The chrysanthemum is the birth flower for the month of November. Aligned with the Sun and the element of Fire, this hardy perennial is a staple of the autumn garden. Among its many magical qualities, the "mum," as its often called, can repel ghosts from the home. Gather some mums from the garden and fill up a vase in your house. Enchant the flowers with a little help from the waning Moon with the following verse to help keep discontented spirits at bay. Work this spell at sunset to bring in the closing energies of the day.

The chrysanthemum is a flower of November,

Lend your magic to mine, come what ever.

All spirits not in alignment with me must depart,

Hear me now as I work my witch's art.

Allow the flowers to work their magic until they begin to fade. Then neatly return them to nature.

Ellen Dugan

Notes:

November 10
Saturday

4th ♏
☽ → ♎ 4:35 am

Color of the day: Blue
Incense of the day: Sage

Renewal Ritual

As the days grow shorter and darker and the nights grow longer, many of us feel blue. We miss summer's warm energy and can be physically affected by the declining amount of sunlight. If you are feeling a little blue, this simple ritual can help you to recharge and renew.

- Pack a lunch of tuna sandwiches, cheese, and soymilk or milk.

- Dress warmly. Take your midday lunch outdoors somewhere that you can sit in the Sun.

- Turn to face the Sun, and feel its warmth reaching you despite cold weather.

- Eat slowly, knowing that tuna, milk, and soy milk are all high in vitamin D.

And, the combination of natural light and vitamin D will help to put you right. Renew.

Dallas Jennifer Cobb

November 11
Sunday

Veterans Day

4th ♎

Color of the day: Gold
Incense of the day: Marigold

Exploring Worlds within Worlds

Today is Old November day; it's a day to honor the fairy Sidhe, who were considered supernatural beings akin to elves or fairies. Some say they exist in parallel universes or invisible worlds that coexist with our world.

In the morning, burn an incense of dittany of Crete, wormwood, and sandalwood. Meditate on the rising smoke or gaze into a crystal ball. Can you see your ancestors, the Sidhe, or maybe your doppelganger, in an alternate reality? Ask the Sidhe to guide you through the day. Ring a small bell and state aloud:

> Only higher vibrations are welcome here.

Make an offering of a piece of fluorite, or carry it with you during the day. Pay extra attention to any signs or intuitions that come to you. When alone, speak quietly to them and ask questions. Write down your impressions and review them from time to time.

Kelly Proudfoot

November 12
Monday

4th ♎

☽ v/c 12:13 am

☽ → ♏ 6:10 am

Color of the day: Lavender
Incense of the day: Lily

Indian Summer

Many of us refer to sunny autumn weather as "Indian Summer." In truth, Indian summer describes any period of warm weather that follows leaf drop and hard frost but occurs before the first snowfall and between mid October and late November. The term comes from the Native Americans, many of whom believed the warm burst of weather to be a gift of the gods. In some European countries, Indian summer is called Gypsy summer, Old Ladies summer, or Crone's summer, referencing medieval links between weather, folklore, and witches.

Welcome and honor the gift of Indian summer! Throw open the windows to let the fresh, warm air fill your home. Set out a jar of spring water to "charge" under the autumn Sun; use later in spells or blessings or to impart correspondences of benefi-cence, surprise, bounty, or harvest. A piece of wood gifted or discovered at Indian summer makes a powerful wand!

Susan Pesznecker

NOTES:

November 13
Tuesday

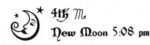

4th ♏

New Moon 5:08 pm

Color of the day: Red
Incense of the day: Ylang-ylang

A New Moon Meditation

The New Moon of November begins a period of transition and introspection. The harvest ends, and we ready ourselves for winter. Although the natural world seems to be dying, it's only dormant. If you look closely at the bare branches of trees and shrubs, you'll notice the buds containing next season's flower and leaf have already been formed. This phase of dormancy shouldn't be mistaken for stagnation. During this New Moon, the Life Force slumbers in the womb of Mother Earth. This should be a time of evaluation and renewal. With the Sun in Scorpio, meditation can be very useful now; here is one example. You'll need:

- one brown candle
- one white candle
- the Four of Swords card from the tarot

In silence, light the candles. The brown candle represents the sleeping, but fertile, Mother Earth. The white candle symbolizes the Divine Spirit, which may be unseen but is always present. Place the Four of Swords card between the candles. This represents a period of contemplation. Sit quietly before the candles until you feel a connection to both Earth and Spirit. Think of a goal you wish to accomplish. As the Moon grows in power, take steps to achieve your goal.

Jim Kambos

NOTES:

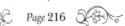

November 14
Wednesday

 1st ♏︎

☽ v/c 5:39 am

☽ → ♐ 5:52 am

Color of the day: Brown
Incense of the day: Lilac

Give It Away

Now is the time to give away a meaningful chunk of your stuff—at least one meaningful item—to Good Will, your sister, best friend, the Earth, or another appropriate receptacle. Think you can't part with it? Well, you can; and for your spiritual growth, you must! Seated in your favorite spot, look around you and think about the things you love the most. Is there a book, an heirloom, a cherished knick-knack that holds a dear place in your heart? Is there something you made (perhaps during a ritual) or had made that brings back special memories? Today, practice the art of non-attachment and make a match between your material good and a beloved person or cause. Let go with celebration and a sense of the freedom the release brings.

Chandra Alexandre

November 15
Thursday

Islamic New Year

 1st ♐

Color of the day: Turquoise
Incense of the day: Clove

A Bottle Spell for Remembrance

This is a spell to honor a special memory, with the intent of "capturing" the moment—or the memory of someone dear to you who has passed on.

Select a picture (or two) that represents the event, if you have one. If not, write a description. Roll the paper and insert it into a bottle. Add three stalks of dried rosemary or three tablespoons of dried rosemary leaves. Seal the bottle, and chant the following:

A special person, place, or time

I honor with this simple rhyme.

May it serve my memory,

And remain a part of me.

Keep the bottle where you can see it.

Ember Grant

November 16
Friday

 1st ♐
)) v/c **4:44 am**

)) → ♑ **5:35 am**

Color of the day: Black
Incense of the day: Ivy

Hecate Night Love Spell

Not everyone wants a traditional wedding or a storybook romance. Some of us prefer a more unique partnership that allows us our fierceness, our so-called "weirdness," and our autonomy. It's Hecate Night. To call on Hecate to help draw and prepare for a partner who's as feisty and free as you are, and who will revel in your creativity and independence, perform this spell.

After dark, by candlelight, place two (naturally shed) black feathers in a red flannel bag. Add a pinch of powdered cloves. Tie it closed with twine as you chant:

> *One is one and two is two*
>
> *Me for me and you for you.*
>
> *When we meet we both shall know*
>
> *For Hecate the way shall show.*

Extinguish the candles and take the charm to a three-way crossroads. Leave it there with an offering to Hecate: a head of garlic and three whole dried star anise fruits.

Tess Whitehurst

NOTES:

November 17

Saturday

1st ♑

Color of the day: Orange
Incense of the day: Frankincense

Sleep Protection Spell

Are you having nightmares or other bad dreams? Create a dream protector. There are many possibilities. I've heard that nutcrackers of the classic sort, that look like old-fashioned toy soldiers, can be used as bedside guardians. Dragons are a protective totem in Asian mythology. Find the image that seems protective to you; this can be a flat picture you can hang on the wall over your bed, or a statue small enough to sit on your bedside table. If you can take it along with you if you sleep somewhere else, that's a plus. Once you have the image chosen, put it on your altar and cast a circle. Bless it with the elements, then invoke the spirit of that figure and ask it to be your dream protector. If you get a positive response from the spirit, thank it, and end the circle. Put the image by your bed, and thank it every morning.

Magenta

November 18
Sunday

1st ♑

☽ v/c 12:54 am

☽ → ♒ 7:10 am

Color of the day: Gray
Incense of the day: Clary sage

Oak Prosperity Spell

Open yourself to success and prosperity by inviting it into your life. You'll need a green candle, some oak leaves and acorns, and a gold-colored coin. (Try a Sacagawea dollar. If you don't have one, try your bank.) On the green candle, carve a straight vertical line, then two short horizontal lines coming out on the left side, one above the other. This is the Ogham symbol for oak, and it speaks of strength, endurance, and honorable opportunities opening before you. Surround the candle with oak leaves and acorns, and set the gold coin in front. Say:

> Mighty spirit of oak, plenty I see as I invite prosperity to come to me.
>
> This shining coin will draw much more,
>
> My needs are met, I open the door.

Light the candle and envision yourself opening to prosperity. When the candle burns down, carry the coin with you and don't spend it.

Mickie Mueller

NOTES:

November 19
Monday

1st ≈

Color of the day: Rose
Incense of the day: Yarrow

Computer healing

One of the most important tools for information and communication can be our computers. We need to keep them healthy and clean if we want these mechanical gnomes to keep serving us faithfully.

Be sure to "defrag" your hard drive regularly. Your antivirus software should be renewed annually and the antivirus definitions files should be updated regularly (if not set to update automatically).

Keep your operating system patched and updated. Be sure you have a good spyware/malware protection program and remover on your computer. Most of these fixes and preventions are cheap or free and can be had by using the great god of searching: Google.

Finally, be sure your computer is kept free from dust in the air intakes and that it is in a cool, dry place. Keep this spell working going on a regular basis to ensure your cyber-gnome will serve you for many years.

Boudica

November 20
Tuesday

1st ♒

☽ v/c 9:31 am

2nd Quarter 9:31 am

☽ → ♓ 11:55 am

Color of the day: Scarlet
Incense of the day: Cinnamon

Keep Away Spell

Each of us has people or things that really rattle our chains and seem to disrespect our space. A simple spell of "Keep Away" can help us change their behaviors. First, make a poppet of yourself. Build a structure to represent the space you feel you need to keep safe. Popsicle sticks are good to work with, but pebbles or stones can also be used to create a stronghold. Determine how much protection you want to use. With permanent marker, write KEEP AWAY on the outside of the structure. Place your poppet inside the structure and loudly say:

Hear me now, my will obey

You are not welcome,

KEEP AWAY.

When you see the person, repeat the chant quietly to yourself. Also practice in front of a mirror, repeating the chant. Notice your body language.

Stand straight, square your shoulders, keep your feet firmly balanced, and let your entire body reinforce your thoughts.

Paniteowl

Notes:

November 21
Wednesday

 2nd ♓

☉ → ♐ 4:50 pm

Color of the day: White
Incense of the day: Marjoram

Spell for Positive Energy

The Sun enters the sign of the archer today. Sagittarius is considered a "masculine" sign; it is also a mutable sign. Sagittarius is ruled by the planet Jupiter. The color associated with Sagittarius is purple. The strengths of Sagittarius include a positive outlook on life energy, adventure, and versatility. Let's tap into the power of the waxing Moon and this zodiac-sign energy, and pull some magic into your life. Light a purple candle and repeat the charm. This spell will compliment all astrological signs.

> The purple candle now burns
> to honor the archer's design.
>
> Bring adventure and versatility
> swiftly to me,
>
> And please bless me with
> positive magical energy.

By the stars above me, this spell is spun,

For the good of all and with harm to none.

Allow the candle to burn out in a safe place.

Ellen Dugan

NOTES:

 Page 223

November 22
Thursday
Thanksgiving Day

 2nd ♓
☽ v/c 1:32 am
☽ → ♈ 8:12 pm
Color of the day: Green
Incense of the day: Nutmeg

Giving Thanks

As we celebrate Thanksgiving by eating turkey and pumpkin pie, we often forget the most important part of this holiday—giving thanks. People everywhere, not just in the United States, can set aside time out on this day to count blessings and remember how lucky we are. No matter how rough our lives are, there is always someone who is worse off. It's easy to lose track of the many good things in our lives and focus only on the bad. Make a list of all your blessings—large and small— and thank the gods for the gifts they have given you. If you want, you can recite this short prayer:

*God and Goddess, I thank you
for the blessings of my life*

And for your presence within me.

May my blessings continue and multiply

And may I never take them for granted.

Deborah Blake

NOTES:

 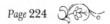

November 23
Friday

2nd ♈

☽ v/c 8:34 pm

Color of the day: Purple
Incense of the day: Thyme

Enchant Your Computer Spell

If you use a computer, this quick spell may be for you. Begin by anointing yourself with ground cinnamon powder; rub it on your chest, legs, arms, and neck. Cinnamon is aligned to Mercury. Approach your computer and draw the symbol for Mercury on the computer with your finger. With a ballpoint pen, draw the symbol on both of your hands, symbolizing the connection between your hands and the computer. Gaze at the screen and say:

> Holy Mercury, messenger of the gods, divine communicator!
>
> I ask that you bless this instrument of communication and knowledge.
>
> May I give and receive the knowledge of the Universe through this device,

And may my interactions be only of a positive and progressive nature.

As I will, so mote it be!

Raven Digitalis

NOTES:

November 24
Saturday

2nd ♈

Color of the day: Brown
Incense of the day: Pine

Spell for Unity

Use this spell to bring unity to a family gathering or to create a feeling of closeness for a family that can't be physically together. This can also be used for groups of close friends. At the dinner table or other place where the group would gather, arrange candles in a circle, one for each person you wish to include. Place a quartz crystal cluster inside the ring of candles. As you light the candles, repeat this chant:

> Gather us together here
>
> Both from far away, and near
>
> Link our lives and join our hearts
>
> While together and apart.

> Ember Grant

November 25
Sunday

2nd ♈

☽ → ♉ 7:18 am

Color of the day: Yellow
Incense of the day: Heliotrope

Grounded in Abundance Ritual

To anchor yourself in an earthy feeling of abundance, so that you begin to attract wealth and blessings as a matter of course, perform this ritual. This is also great for anytime you need help sleeping, or if you feel too airy, spacey, wishy-washy, or generally ungrounded.

Obtain a brown cloth that is about the size of the top of your mattress. Remove your mattress and spread the cloth over your box spring. On top, sprinkle a tiny bit of a mixture of patchouli powder and cinnamon as you chant:

> Abundance of the land abounds,
>
> From light above and holy ground.
>
> Healthy, wealthy, joyful, blessed,
>
> Divinely anchored as I rest.

Hold your hands in prayer pose, close your eyes, and envision the cloth swirling and pulsating with the sparkly-brown, fertile, grounding light of the Earth. Replace the mattress, so that the cloth remains sandwiched between the mattress and box spring.

Tess Whitehurst

NOTES:

November 26
Monday

2nd ♉
☽ v/c 7:57 pm

Color of the day: Lavender
Incense of the day: Hyssop

Fear Not the Dark

St. Peter of Alexandria, a bishop during the reign of Emperor Diocletian, guarded his flock against religious persecution. He hid and protected them, and taught them to 'fear not' death, for only through death is there resurrection. In 311 CE, St. Peter was captured, tortured, and put to death without succumbing to fear.

Today, fear not. Write a simple list of what you fear. Is it poverty? Homelessness? Illness or death? Take a note from St. Peter, and fear not. Face your fears, and know that deep inside you have his saintly powers to protect yourself and your faith. Renounce your need to dwell only in light. Allow yourself to slip into darkness with the season, and know your fears. This natural cycle of birth, life, death, and rebirth is continually at play, and only through death, as we see in the plants now, will rebirth in spring be possible.

Dallas Jennifer Cobb

November 27
Tuesday

2nd ♉
☽ → ♊ 7:58 pm

Color of the day: Gray
Incense of the day: Bay laurel

Stop the Gossip Spell

If you're a victim of gossip or rumor, this spell will help remove the power of the rumor, and destroy it. You'll need some gray stationery, a gray envelope, and a gray candle. The color gray is used in this spell to neutralize any negativity, without creating bad karma for you. Light the candle first. Then write a description of the gossip on the stationery, and declare that you wish to stop it without hurting anyone. Even if you know who started the rumor, don't mention them. Then fold the stationery and seal it in the envelope. Ignite the envelope in the candle flame, and let everything burn in a heat-proof container. As it burns, say:

Talk is cheap, talk is trash,

Lies and rumors be turned to ash!

When the ashes cool, scatter them outside after dark. The gossip will end without harming you or anyone else.

James Kambos

November 28
Wednesday

2nd ♊
Full Moon 9:46 am

☽ v/c 8:04 pm

Color of the day: Yellow
Incense of the day: Lavender

Full Moon Spell

During this Full Moon, communication is everything. Over the upcoming holidays, communicating with eloquence and grace honors those whom you care about. Arrange a bouquet of white carnations representing bonds of affection and pure love; add a few ferns for sincerity. Place the flowers in the best vase you own; if it's a family heirloom, all the better. If you haven't sent out your holiday cards, you may wish to have them nearby to bless them. Anoint the base of your neck and the center of your forehead with lavender oil, light a white candle, and think joyful thoughts. As you ask the Moon Goddess to guide you through holiday gatherings and communications, say:

Shining Lady Moon of my being

Unto the divine within,

Walk with me during the month ahead,

Help me to act with honor

And to speak with honor

In all that I do.

*Help me to walk in your love
and your light*

*With grace, dignity, and
wisdom.*

Keep the bouquet in your home for
as long as it lasts. Before you attend
any gatherings or write your cards
during the upcoming month, anoint
the base of your neck with lavender
oil again, and communicate with love
and honor.

Mickie Mueller

NOTES:

November 29
Thursday

3rd ♊

Color of the day: White
Incense of the day: Jasmine

A Day of Beauty

Surround yourself with beautiful
things today in honor of Hathor
in her triple goddess form along
with Bast and Sekhmet. Take a long,
luxurious bath or shower and use the
time to beautify yourself. Wear exotic
jewelry and whatever makes you feel
lovely!

Drink wine and celebrate the
goddesses by offering a glass. Make
music by beating a tambourine or
singing and dancing. Adorn your
sacred space with flowers and gems.
Burn frankincense, myrrh, and dragonsblood in honor of the goddesses.
Carry a piece of tiger's-eye, and
express your creativity by painting or
sketching something.

Put a few drops of ylang-ylang
or sandalwood in your oil burner
and enjoy the scent. Make love and
feel the intoxication of the moment.
However you do it (alone or otherwise!), feel the power of the feminine
within you. Allow yourself to be free,
and thank the triple goddess for the
energies!

Kelly Proudfoot

November 30
Friday

 3rd ♊
☽ → ♋ 8:55 am

Color of the day: White
Incense of the day: Violet

holidays from the heart

We stand on the brink of December's holiday season, a joyful season of light and life: Plan ahead to enjoy it fully! Begin by considering which parts of the holiday season are important to you and your family. Put these at the top of the list and get rid of anything that doesn't add to your celebration. Spread activities out over the month. Embrace the built-in peacefulness of the season: Turn off cell phone, computer, and television and spend quiet time with the lights or by the fire, contemplating the quiet depths of late autumn. Take walks at sunrise or sunset— liminal times for experiencing the season's magic. Feed the birds. Read a new book or play board games with your family. Study a new magical idea, craft a new tool, or work with divination. Begin and end each day with a moment of calm mindfulness, incanting *ex animo*: "from the heart."

Susan Pesznecker

NOTES:

December

December is a wonder FULL month! Bright sunlight on glistening snow that fills us with magical wonder can turn into a blizzard, or to slushy, slippery roads that make our hearts leap into our throats! Yet we embrace this month of extreme changes. The Solstice will arrive, and we will renew the cycle of contemplation and new expectations. For many Pagans, this "winding down" of the old year encourages us to finish things we started and get our affairs in order. We look to the promise of the Sun's returning, of days getting longer, and new possibilities hovering on the horizon. We celebrate this renewal by getting together with family and friends and sharing our optimism for the coming year. Sometimes, the magic of December gets lost in a flurry of shopping, planning, and parties that have little to do with our religious beliefs, but we can't ignore the special feelings that pervade the spirit of the season during this magical month. It is the time of year that most strongly calls to us to remember our past and celebrate our future in tune with the cycles of nature. It can be harsh. But, more often, December nurtures our inner child to explore and embrace the hope and possibilities of life ahead of us.

Paniteowl

December 1
Saturday

 3rd ♋

Color of the day: Ivory
Incense of the day: Blue

Poinsettia Spell

In the language of flowers, the red poinsettia symbolizes "be of good cheer." I assign the planetary association of the Sun and the element of Fire to this native Central American plant. As December begins, we can liven up our homes with a live plant to help celebrate the winter holidays. The plant can be enchanted to banish the blues, and to radiate out cheer and happiness with the following flower fascination.

With the power of the waning Moon, I banish the blues,

Now I quickly bring forth good cheer and happiness so true.

With a touch of color magic, now brighten up these days,

By leaf and flower, change moods in the best possible way.

Place the poinsettia plant in a prominent place, keep it well cared for, and enjoy the magic!

Ellen Dugan

December 2
Sunday

 3rd ♋
☽ v/c 1:55 am

☽ → ♌ 8:57 pm

Color of the day: Yellow
Incense of the day: Eucalyptus

An Astral Travel Exercise

There are many ways to do astral projection, and it's a good idea to research the subject. Try this exercise and practice whenever you have quiet time. First, fill a white mojo bag with poplar, jasmine, and mugwort along with a piece of fluorite. Anoint it with Astral Oil, made as follows:

> 2 drops each of jasmine, sandalwood, cinnamon
>
> 1 drop ylang-ylang
>
> 4 drops almond oil

Also use the oil to anoint the chakra points from the feet to the crown. When you won't be disturbed, lie down and clench, then release, each muscle, in turn, from your feet to your scalp. As you work your way up, visualize each chakra opening up and spinning clockwise.

 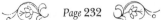

Then, focus on seeing yourself from outside your body, from the corner of the room. Imagine Bast in black panther form watching over your physical body while you travel. Keep practicing!

Kelly Proudfoot

NOTES:

December 3
Monday

3rd ♌

Color of the day: Silver
Incense of the day: Clary sage

A Spell for Balance

A healthy balance of emotions is vital for our overall mental and physical health. To help keep the balance, use this candle spell to minimize any pain you're experiencing and draw in more joy. Always remember to seek medical help if you face issues you can't overcome. Asking for help shows strength and the ability to know oneself.

> By the light of Moon and Sun,
>
> By my words this spell begun:
>
> As I spark this candle flame,
>
> May the light dispel my pain.
>
> By the light of Moon and Sun,
>
> By my words this spell begun:
>
> As this candle burns away
>
> Happiness will come my way.

Ember Grant

December 4
Tuesday

 3rd ♌
☽ v/c 5:08 pm

Color of the day: Red
Incense of the day: Basil

Reasonable Expectations Spell

As we enter the holiday season, many folks find themselves depressed rather than joyous. One of the reasons for this is that it is hard to have reasonable expectations of the people and the season, and so we find ourselves disappointed and let-down. Try doing this spell for balance and a less unsettled attitude, to keep yourself on a more even keel. Light a blue candle. Burn some lavender incense and say:

Tis the season to be jolly

Full of mistletoe and holly

Let my expectations be

As healthy as a living tree

Hope that soars, fine and free

*And roots to ground
and center me*

*Bless me with both joy
and reason*

As I celebrate the season

Deborah Blake

December 5
Wednesday

 3rd ♌
☽ → ♍ 6:51 am

Color of the day: Brown
Incense of the day: Marjoram

Faunalia (Roman god Faunus)

The holiday of Faunalia was set aside for worship of the Roman god Faunus. He rules over fields and shepherds, also the art of prophecy. He is associated with woodpeckers, rain, and the wilderness. Faunus can grant virility or fertility, and luck in the pursuit of carnal pleasures (though not so much with romance). Traditionally celebrated in rural areas, this holiday features feasting and dances performed in triple measure. Now is a good time for bed-sports that are free of romantic entanglements. To seek a casual lover today, anoint yourself with essential oil that has a musky or woodsy fragrance. Then pray to Faunus:

As the horny ram to the ewe,

Make me virile in all that I do.

As the wooly ewe to the ram,

Make me sexy in all that I am.

Faunus of field and wild wood,

Pray let my lust-hunting be good!

Indulge responsibly and remember to take precautions.

Elizabeth Barrette

NOTES:

December 6
Thursday

3rd ♏

4th Quarter 10:31 am

Color of the day: Green
Incense of the day: Carnation

Bast Blessing

I am blessed by the companionship of three cats, and I know that cats practice a lot of powerful magic. When it is cold at night and a cat snuggles next to me, it lifts my spirits. Magic! Today, bless your cats, the animals who bless you, with this small spell. Fill their water and food dishes, and say:

> *I bless you with nutrition and health.*

Clean out the litter box and say:

> *I bless you with cleanliness and care,*

Afterward, snuggle your cat and as you pat it say:

> *I am blessed by Bast, the great wise Cat*

> *I am blessed by cat, the great wise Bast*

> *Bast be blessed, cat be blessed,*

> *Bless you Bast, and Bless you cat.*

Dallas Jennifer Cobb

December 7
Friday

 4th ♏
☽ v/c 5:35 am
☽ → ♎ 1:35 pm

Color of the day: Pink
Incense of the day: Vanilla

Be honey-Intoxicated!

In ancient Greece, the phrase "honey-intoxicated" meant to be drunk. Today, we call on the Melissae—the bee priestesses—to offer us their gifts of sweet prophecy so that we may learn the secrets of becoming drunk on life. Bring to your altar or a garden spot a small pot of honey and a cherished book. Tapping into your connection with the Divine, invoke the Melissae and ask that they come to you now. Open your heart to the depths of your soul and therein seek potentials for fulfillment under the Melissae's watchful guidance. Taking a taste of honey with your right index finger, close your eyes, open the book, and let your finger rest on a word or picture. Repeat this six times, the sacred number of the bee goddess, and take in the message delivered through this oracle.

Chandra Alexandre

December 8
Saturday

4th ♎
☽ v/c 7:37 pm

Color of the day: Black
Incense of the day: Patchouli

Sadie, Goddess of Bargain Shoppers

Sadie, Sadie, bargain shopping lady, what treasures can you find for me?

Sadie is telling you to get out early this year and get those gifts before Yule. Don't put it off. There are some great bargains to be had if you get out and get it done now!

Go to the mall or your favorite department store and look for Sadie. She is the smart-looking, gray-haired lady who is weighed down with bulging shopping bags. Watch the stores she enters, or the departments she visits, and keep behind her as she stops at shelves, bins, and displays. Give a stop at those as well, looking for those perfect gifts for your friends and family. You will be surprised at the discounts and bargains you will find!

Listen to your secret goddess and get out and get it done now. And don't forget the wrapping paper!

Boudica

December 9
Sunday
hanukkah begins

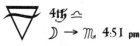

Color of the day: Gold
Incense of the day: Frankincense

No Regrets Amethyst Spell

Sometimes it's easy for us to get a little too merry during the holidays, either with tempting treats or with spirits. If you feel the need for a little magic to help you celebrate the season without the excess, here is a simple spell for you. You'll need a piece of amethyst; it can be a tumbled stone, but a piece of jewelry is even better. Hold the stone in your hand and repeat:

Help me stick to moderation,

Strength when faced with temptation,

The smartest choices shall I make

To each decision, I'm wide awake.

Bring your amethyst charm with you to every celebration, and make it a reminder of your promise to yourself. Decide before you go what your limits are, and stick to them. Make sure you treat yourself, just in moderation.

Mickie Mueller

NOTES:

December 10
Monday

4th ♏

Color of the day: Lavender
Incense of the day: Hyssop

Dream Journal

With the long nights this time of year, consider recording your dreams in a dream journal. Some people like a small bound journal, others a large notebook. Loose sheets of paper are fine too, perhaps on a clipboard, or in a loose-leaf notebook. Lined paper may be easier for words. Unlined paper is easier to draw on, though; it's specially useful for dreams, which may have images there are no words to describe. A pencil lets you erase mistakes, which I find more common when I've just woken up. Colored pencils or markers let you not only draw but add colors. Whatever you use, keep it by the bed if you can, so you can record dreams as soon as you wake up. A small light, like a book light, may be useful if you share a bed. If necessary, keep your dream journal in the bathroom or another room, so as not to wake up others.

Magenta

December 11
Tuesday

4th ♏
☽ v/c 8:08 am
☽ → ♐ 5:22 pm

Color of the day: Red
Incense of the day: Cinnamon

Simple Spirit–Clearing Ritual

Do you suspect that your home harbors confused, unfriendly, and/or stubborn spirits hovering in limbo between this realm and the next? If so, today's a great day to persuade them to get out. Even if there aren't any spirits hanging around, this simple ritual will help lift the vibes and clear the space for positive energy and conditions.

Fill a bowl with a mixture of sea salt, powdered garlic, and powdered sage. Place a white candle in the middle. Place the bowl in the middle of a room and light the candle. Move around the room in a counterclockwise direction while burning a bundle of sage (with dish). Move the bowl to another room and repeat. Repeat in all rooms and areas. Extinguish the candle and flush the salt mixture down the toilet.

Note: for especially stubborn spirits, you might need to repeat the ritual, or do a different one.

Tess Whitehurst

December 12
Wednesday

 4th ♐

Color of the day: Yellow
Incense of the day: Lavender

A Spell for the Lonely

During the excitement of the holiday season it's easy to forget that many people find this to be the loneliest time of the year. To help someone cope with loneliness and depression during the Yuletide season, say words of power and ask that you'll find an appropriate way to bring cheer to someone in need. Think of people you may help. Do you know someone who has suffered the loss of a loved one, is recently divorced, or is unemployed? Instead of buying them a gift, invite them to take part in one of your holiday activities. Perhaps you could ask them over for an afternoon of holiday cooking or baking. Or, just invite them for tea and conversation. If you know someone who's ill, offer to do some of their holiday shopping, decorate their home, wrap their gifts, or just visit. Whatever you do, your actions will create good karma, which helps everyone.

James Kambos

NOTES:

December 13
Thursday

 4th ♐
𝒩ew 𝒨oon 3:42 am

☽ → ♑ 4:43 pm

Color of the day: Turquoise
Incense of the day: Balsam

The Golden Lights of St. Lucia

In Sweden, December 13 is Santa Lucia Day, a nationwide festival of light in which a young girl in a flowing white gown serves guests coffee and lussebulle or lussekatter (saffron buns) in the early morning. Lussekatter is an ancient reference to Lucifer, who would appear in the shape of a cat to spirit children away. The buns also represent the Sun's power as it returns after the solstice, referencing success, prosperity, and growth. Create your own lussekatter using pre-made sweet bread dough. Saffron traditionally imparts a rich gold color to the rolls, but it's the world's most expensive spice; instead, knead in some yellow food-color paste (from the baking aisle) to create a Sun-like gold hue. Shape each roll into a spiral or the customary "reverse S," or create round orbs to honor the returning Sun. Brush with butter and sprinkle with cinnamon, sugar, and ground cardamom before baking; this further honors the solar correspondences and tastes delicious, too! Today is the New Moon, and your "saffron buns" will work beautifully as the cakes and ale for your New Moon esbat. Serve the lussekatter on dark plates and offer spiced red wine as an accompaniment, echoing the Dark Moon.

Susan Pesznecker

NOTES:

December 14
Friday

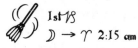 1st ♑

☽ → ♈ 2:15 am

Color of the day: Coral
Incense of the day: Orchid

Clear Your Energy

Coming in from the cold, there is nothing quite so comforting as a long warm bath. Epsom salt, composed of magnesium and sulfate, has healing properties that positively affect the body, mind, and spirit. Magnesium can be depleted from the body by stress, so soaking in Epsom salt helps to antidote this. It draws toxins from the body, soothes the nervous system, reduces physical swelling, and relaxes muscles. Magnesium also helps to produce serotonin within the brain, a mood-elevating chemical that produces calm, good feelings. This purification bath will cleanse residual negative energy from your physical body, calm you emotionally, uplift your mental state, and clear spiritual and etheric bodies.

Purification Bath

In the tub, dissolve in hot running water:

2 cups of Epsom salt

15 drops of lavender essential oil

Slip in and soak with your eyes closed, feeling the stress ease from your body, and your spirits elevate.

Dallas Jennifer Cobb

NOTES:

 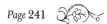

December 15
Saturday

 1st ♑

☽ v/c 4:15 pm

☽ → ≈ 4:53 pm

Color of the day: Brown
Incense of the day: Pine

honey Jar Sweetening Spell

This spell has its roots in hoodoo and conjure magic, which carries a heavy element of "folk" spellcraft and superstition. Because honey is a naturally sweet substance, it can be used in magic to help sweeten up a bitter person or situation. Honey is also physically used for healing, meaning that it also carries metaphysical healing properties. If there is a person or situation that requires healing or sweetening, simply write their name or a description of the situation on a piece of paper. If appropriate, include a photograph or something belonging to the person (or from a property or from a time in your life, or what have you), and anything else to energetically link to the purpose. In a small jar filled with honey, insert the items and cap the jar. Gazing at the items in the jar, visualize the target sweetening up and/or healing. Say some positive affirmations out loud and incorporate the jar into any additional spell craft you'd like. Place the jar on an altar or in the back of a closet (so the honey won't get eaten!). This spell can sit for as long as need be, so when you feel the magic has worked, just toss the jar in the trash.

Raven Digitalis

NOTES:

December 16
Sunday

hanukkah ends

1st ♒

Color of the day: Amber
Incense of the day: Hydrangea

Find Me Spell

Sometimes I think that car keys, change purses, and things I've put away so that I won't lose them are conspiring to drive me crazy. They always hide when I need them most and I'm in a hurry. I've used the "Find Me" spell so often that my pendulum automatically starts "searching" when I bring out my drawing! Use a large piece of graph paper and draw a schematic of your home. Draw another graph of your neighborhood, another of your car, and another of your workplace. Place one of the graphs on a table, and holding your pendulum steady in your "sending" hand (right hand if you're right-handed, left if you're left-handed) and say out loud, "Find me the object that I need, quickly seek with skill and speed" … then say the name of the object three times. If your pendulum fails to move, choose another of the graphs until you get a response. Move the pendulum over the graph until it pinpoints an area for you to consider. Search that area, and when you find your item, come back to the graph and gently stroke the pendulum until it remains stationery. Thank the pendulum for its help and put it away someplace safe so that you will find it the next time you need it. (You might want to have two pendulums, just so one can help you find the other!)

Paniteowl

NOTES:

December 17
Monday

1st ♒

☽ v/c 1:12 pm

☽ → ♓ 7:48 pm

Color of the day: White
Incense of the day: Rosemary

Saturnalia Begins

Today marks the beginning of the Roman celebration of Saturnalia, one of the roots of the Christmas celebration. This festival lasted about a week. It was intended to honor the god Saturn and included giving gifts and general merrymaking, in addition to role reversal. To kick off your season of holiday celebrations, make Saturnalia gifts for your friends and family members.

In many cultures, boughs of evergreen represent everlasting life. Create mini boughs of pine, cedar, and holly to hang in the home. Tie them together with red ribbon and decorate them as you choose. Attach a tag with the following message to each one you give away, offering blessings for the season.

Blessings for your home and hearth,

Joyful times of love and warmth.

Family and friends be near,

Wishing you delight and cheer.

Ember Grant

NOTES:

December 18
Tuesday

 1st ♓

Color of the day: Black
Incense of the day: Ginger

Festival of Epona: Goddess of horses

Epona became known throughout the ancient world after she was adopted by the Roman cavalry. Horses, of course a chief part of war strategies then, are known for their nobility, strength, grace, and power. Each of these characteristics provides keys to happiness, and it is with this in mind that we surround ourselves today with Epona's mantle. Also a goddess of fertility, worship of Epona brings possibilities for new life. To celebrate her, bring together an apple, some nuts, pine or cedar incense, cider, water, and salt. Purify with water and salt, then salt the apple, light incense, and raise a glass to the Great Mare, saying, "Epona Reginae!" to call her Queen. Pray to her for your journeys in this life, for safe passage to the other world, for travels near and far, and for fruitful new beginnings.

Chandra Alexandre

December 19
Wednesday

 1st ♓

Color of the day: Topaz
Incense of the day: Honeysuckle

Clearing the Sate

Use today to tie up loose ends for the year. Make a list of anything you feel needs to be finalized before you enter the new year. Did you leave any arguments unresolved? Have you ignored or hurt anyone's feelings this year? Has anyone crossed you?

Write sincere apology letters and bridge the gaps by expressing your true feelings. After doing this, light a green candle anointed with olive oil and consecrated to Mercury. Say aloud:

> Hail to thee, Mercury.
> Please help me with my plight.
>
> I'm making amends, tying up
> loose ends,
>
> Help my messages take flight!

Let the candle burn down with the letters close by. When you send them, carry a green mojo bag of violet, skullcap, and lemongrass. Visualize a dove with an olive twig following at Mercury's heels to ensure that your letters are received with love and understanding.

Kelly Proudfoot

December 20
Thursday

 1st ♓

☽ v/c 12:19 am

2nd Quarter 12:19 am

☽ → ♈ 2:43 am

Color of the day: Green

Incense of the day: Apricot

holly and Ivy Spell

The holly and ivy are plants also assigned to the birth month of December. Holly's qualities are of Mars and Fire, white ivy is Saturn and Water—they are a perfect December combination. Add a touch of nature's magic to your home this holiday season and enjoy the positive, joyful, and protective qualities of these plants. (For safety, please be sure and keep fresh holly berries out of reach of small children and pets.)

Holly and ivy are plants full of magical lore,

They will bring protection and charm as in days of yore.

Now guard well my home, bring us all good cheer and holiday fun,

While we look forward to the return of the newly born Sun.

You may leave the greenery in place until the Yuletide season ends. Then add it to your yard waste to be recycled.

Ellen Dugan

NOTES:

December 21
Friday

Yule – Winter Solstice

 2nd ♈

☉ → ♑ 6:12 am

Color of the day: Purple
Incense of the day: Yarrow

Yule Celebration of Abundance and Change

This Yule our focus is an end of an era and the start of a new, brighter future. We welcome the return of the Sun and focus on positive business ventures and change.

The Sun entering Capricorn gives the business-minded a jump-start on abundance. We celebrate this Yule with abundance on the financial, the physical, and the spiritual levels. As we plan our rituals for this holiday, we should concentrate on success, richness in our lives, and positive emphasis for the coming seasons.

We can bring bright-yellow Suns into our home décor and add gold decorated ornaments to increase the feeling of abundance. We can ask Saturn, the ruling planet of Capricorn, for guidance in our planning to become financially sound.

Finally, we can be prepared for change. Grab hold of change and ride it for all it's worth, as this coming year will bring much change to all phases of our lives.

Boudica

NOTES:

December 22
Saturday

2nd ♈︎

☽ v/c 7:57 am

☽ → ♉︎ 1:25 pm

Color of the day: Blue
Incense of the day: Sandalwood

Lighting the Mystery:
A Yule Feast

Today, we turn our attention to the celebration of illumination, to the joys of Yuletide, and to the season of family, food, and laughter. While you may prepare or join in a feast for friends and loved ones, take stock today too of your connection to Spirit, to that unseen feast we can nevertheless find everywhere and in everything. Allow yourself a moment to reflect on all the rays of light brought to your daily life this past year, to your personal awakenings and to your moments of discovery and triumph. Feel today the warmth of new possibilities for your unfolding story, and set a sacred intention for the next turn in the Wheel of the Year. Pause and breathe in through all your senses. Light a white candle, give thanks, and take in the beauty of the Great Mystery.

Chandra Alexandre

December 23
Sunday

2nd ♉︎

Color of the day: Orange
Incense of the day: Almond

Wrap It Up Spell

It's almost Christmas and you still don't have your gift wrapping done. Don't panic, this spell will help, and as a bonus your wrapping will be magically charged too. Assemble your supplies, then your gifts. Set the mood by lighting a holiday scented candle, or simmering some potpourri. Begin by selecting a gift to wrap and think about its recipient. What kind of year have they had? What would you like your gift to convey? Select the paper, and as you cut it, truly feel that you're giving a bit of yourself along with the gift. As you wrap, tape, and tie the ribbon, feel that you're bonding with the recipient. If you're using gift bags and tissue, feel that you're gently surrounding the gift with love. Finish by adding a magical touch. For example, a pine cone is a sign of life and fertility, and a small bell will attract positive spiritual energy, and so on.

James Kambos

December 24
Monday
Christmas Eve

2nd ♉

Color of the day: Gray
Incense of the day: Neroli

A Blessing for Stockings

A widespread European tradition calls for hanging stockings from the mantelpiece on Christmas Eve. Originally just everyday socks, these have evolved into specially decorated sock-shaped bags. The holiday spirit (Santa Claus, St. Nicholas, Frau Holle, Odin, etc.) leaves small gifts, fruit, or money in the stockings. Those who behave well receive the most and best gifts. Those who behave badly may receive nothing, or only a lump of coal. This fits with many historic fairy tales that encourage dutiful behavior. Here is a blessing to say while hanging stockings. It touches on the tradition of almsgiving at Christmas, taking care of the less fortunate. This is ideal if you make donations to charity at this time.

I've been good

And I've done right;

Fill my sock

With treats tonight.

One more thing

I ask of you:

Fill the poor

Folks' stockings too.

Elizabeth Barrette

NOTES:

December 25
Tuesday
Christmas Day

 2nd ♉
☽ v/c 12:58 am

☽ → ♊ 2:13 am

Color of the day: Maroon
Incense of the day: Ylang-ylang

Meditation on Imperfection

We tend to love perfection, perhaps too much. We love the new, the flawless, the ideal. But much of life is imperfect, and anyway, perfection is hard to maintain. We keep the coffee mug with a chip, because our best friend gave it to us; we wear the sweater with a small stain because it was knit by an aunt, just for us. We need to learn the value of imperfections. The Japanese call these *wabi sabi*, and value these items, because they show the transitory nature of the physical world. Characteristics of the *wabi sabi* aesthetic include asymmetry, simplicity, modesty, intimacy, and the suggestion of natural processes. Nature is imperfect, so why should humans, who are part of nature, try to be other than what we are? Cherish limitations, for as the frame defines the picture, so our limits define our lives.

Magenta

December 26
Wednesday
Kwanzaa begins

 2nd ♊

Color of the day: Brown
Incense of the day: Lilac

Transmutation of the Extras

This holiday season, you almost certainly received at least a few things that you don't love, don't need, or won't use. You also very likely received some new things that made your old things less desirable. Today, perform a little classic alchemy and transmute this base metal into gold. Here's how:

Assemble your unwanted gifts and newly unwanted old stuff that's being replaced by the new. Inwardly express gratitude for receiving and/or using these items, then acknowledge that they don't serve you, and do not represent wealth to you.

Now, box (or bag) them up with the loving intention to give them as a gift to an organization of your choice. With joy in your heart, see them no longer as junk to you, but as wealth and blessings to someone else. As soon as you can, donate them, knowing that what you give out comes back to you multiplied.

Tess Whitehurst

December 27
Thursday

 2nd ♊

☽ v/c 1:50 am

☽ → ♋ 3:06 pm

Color of the day: Crimson
Incense of the day: Nutmeg

Mother's Night

Mother's Night celebrates the female life force that anchors winter and sees the return of light and life to the world. Whether honoring the Saxon Modranicht (Mother Night), the Celtic Cailleach, the Norse Frigg, the Scandinavian Skadi, the Germanic Holda, or any number of goddess traditions, all link women and birth to the winter season and the return of the light.

Create a shrine for your favorite winter mother. Create an enclosing ring with pieces of white yarn (for snow) or raffia. Sprinkle with glitter and set candles on the edges. Place your favorite winter goddess figure or effigy in the center—a photograph will do nicely. Use this as a focus for your winter magics and for heightened awareness of the darkness and rebirth inherent in the season. Incant *ex mater* ("from the mother") as you ask the Mother's blessings on your home for the year to come.

Susan Pesznecker

December 28
Friday

 2nd ♋
☽ Full Moon 5:21 am

☽ v/c 9:43 am

Color of the day: Pink
Incense of the day: Cypress

Letting Go

We are at the end of another year and heading into the dark and quiet winter season. Even in those places where it doesn't get cold and dismal, there is a shift to a more internal energy and a slower pace. Take this opportunity to let go of all the things from the year behind you that no longer serve a purpose, so you can go into the dark free and clear and come out the other side ready to create a happy and prosperous new year. Sit in a darkened room and light one white candle. Meditate for a while on which things still bring something positive to your life, and which ones only drag you down. Then say:

God and Goddess,

Help me to let go of the past

And embrace the future

In a bright and positive fashion

And without any old baggage

So mote it be

Deborah Blake

NOTES:

December 29
Saturday

3rd ♋

Color of the day: Gray
Incense of the day: Pine

Rekindle Your Love

We sometimes get so busy this time of year that we don't slow down enough to spend time with our "special someone" and let them know that we appreciate them. Make plans this winter evening for just the two of you, and break down the busy walls between you. In a large pan, add 2 quarts of apple cider and a dash of salt. In tea ball, place 1 teaspoon whole allspice, 1 teaspoon whole cloves, ⅛ teaspoon nutmeg, and a cinnamon stick broken up. Add the tea ball to the pan and bring to a boil, reduce heat and simmer for 20 minutes. While it cooks, stir clockwise concentrating on your loving feelings for your special someone. When you hand your loved one the cup, tell them:

> Apple and spices to warm our hearts,
>
> As we kindle the evening with a new start.

Share it along with some popcorn and a favorite movie.

Mickie Mueller

December 30
Sunday

3rd ♋
☽ → ♌ 2:45 am

Color of the day: Orange
Incense of the day: Heliotrope

Icicle Magic to Banish Pain

This spell assumes that the reader lives in a climate that is currently snowy and cold. If icicles are unavailable, just substitute an ice cube for the spell! This working is used to help banish pain from your life. Taking an icicle, hold it to your chest, thinking about any painful or tormenting situations in your life. See the icicle as a knife in your chest, causing you pain and misery. While you bring the icicle away from your body, consciously intend to banish these things from your life, and think about the various ways you can conquer these situations. Say:

> Cold blade of torment, I cast you away from my sphere! Melt with the season; descend with the snow. I enter healing while this pain flees from my life. So mote it be!

Conclude by melting the icicle in a bowl on your altar overnight. Let the water evaporate over time, dissipating away from you.

Raven Digitalis

December 31
Monday
New Year's Eve

 3rd ♌
☽ v/c 4:52 pm

Color of the day: Ivory
Incense of the day: Neroli

Spell for Financial Assistance

There are plenty of "Money spells" around, and they are quite easy to find, but a "Financial Assistance" spell goes a bit farther. This covers the use of your money, as well as the preservation of your assets. I wish I had worked with this spell a few years ago when my 401K lost 40 percent in a few short months!

Take six bills—$1, $5, 10$, 20$, 50$, 100$—and a picture of your home, car, and any other property you want to preserve. Fasten them together with a safety pin. Put them into a clear jar with a tight lid. Put a green candle on top of the lid, and let it burn, allowing the wax to melt down over the jar. If possible, place the jar with the lit candle in a window where the light of the Full Moon will fall on it. I also suggest placing the jar in a shallow bowl of water just for safety sake. Spread a circle of salt around the jar/bowl and say the following:

I work hard for my money, I save and I plan. I stretch my dollars as far as I can. But this world is changing, and things that I thought were safe and secure have been proven to naught. I need to know more as financial plans crash, so help to keep what is left of my cash!

Now, picture what you need to preserve, and start learning the ways this can be done. Use the Internet, books, local seminars provided by various organizations and companies. Promise yourself that you will first protect your assets, and NEVER gamble on investments with money you can't afford to lose. Keep your jar in your bedroom so that you see it every day when you get up or go to bed. Someday, when you feel financially secure, you will open the jar and treat yourself to something you've been denying yourself. However, if you can, leave it right where it is, and pass the jar, along with the spell working along to your descendants as a way of teaching them a lesson you learned the hard way. Life has a way of throwing you curves, but you can adjust if you focus on your goals.

Paniteowl

Daily Magical Influences

Each day is ruled by a planet that possesses specific magical influences:

Monday (Moon): peace, healing, caring, psychic awareness, and purification.

Tuesday (Mars): passion, sex, courage, aggression, and protection.

Wednesday (Mercury): conscious mind, study, travel, divination, and wisdom.

Thursday (Jupiter): expansion, money, prosperity, and generosity.

Friday (Venus): love, friendship, reconciliation, and beauty.

Saturday (Saturn): longevity, exorcism, endings, homes, and houses.

Sunday (Sun): healing, spirituality, success, strength, and protection.

Lunar Phases

The lunar phase is important in determining best times for magic.

The waxing Moon (from the New Moon to the Full Moon) is the ideal time for magic to draw things toward you.

The Full Moon is the time of greatest power.

The waning Moon (from the Full Moon to the New Moon) is a time for study, meditation, and little magical work (except magic designed to banish harmful energies).

Astrological Symbols

The Sun	☉	Aries	♈
The Moon	☽	Taurus	♉
Mercury	☿	Gemini	♊
Venus	♀	Cancer	♋
Mars	♂	Leo	♌
Jupiter	♃	Virgo	♍
Saturn	♄	Libra	♎
Uranus	♅	Scorpio	♏
Neptune	♆	Sagittarius	♐
Pluto	♇	Capricorn	♑
		Aquarius	♒
		Pisces	♓

The Moon's Sign

The Moon's sign is a traditional consideration for astrologers. The Moon continuously moves through each sign in the zodiac, from Aries to Pisces. The Moon influences the sign it inhabits, creating different energies that affect our daily lives.

Aries: Good for starting things, but lacks staying power. Things occur rapidly, but quickly pass. People tend to be argumentative and assertive.

Taurus: Things begun now do last, tend to increase in value, and become hard to alter. Brings out an appreciation for beauty and sensory experience.

Gemini: Things begun now are easily changed by outside influence. Time for shortcuts, communications, games, and fun.

Cancer: Stimulates emotional rapport between people. Pinpoints need, supports growth and nurturance. Tend to domestic concerns.

Leo: Draws emphasis to the self, to central ideas or institutions, away from connections with others and emotional needs. People tend to be melodramatic.

Virgo: Favors accomplishment of details and commands from higher up. Focus on health, hygiene, and daily schedules.

Libra: Favors cooperation, compromise, social activities, beautification of surroundings, balance, and partnership.

Scorpio: Increases awareness of psychic power. Precipitates psychic crises and ends connections thoroughly. People tend to brood and become secretive under this Moon sign.

Sagittarius: Encourages flights of imagination and confidence. This Moon sign is adventurous, philosophical, and athletic. Favors expansion and growth.

Capricorn: Develops strong structure. Focus on traditions, responsibilities, and obligations. A good time to set boundaries and rules.

Aquarius: Rebellious energy. Time to break habits and make abrupt change. Personal freedom and individuality is the focus.

Pisces: The focus is on dreaming, nostalgia, intuition, and psychic impressions. A good time for spiritual or philanthropic activities.

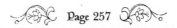

Glossary of Magical Terms

Altar: a low table that holds magical tools as a focus for spell workings.

Athame: a ritual knife used to direct personal power during workings or to symbolically draw diagrams in a spell. It is rarely, if ever, used for actual physical cutting.

Aura: an invisible energy field surrounding a person. The aura can change color depending upon the state of the individual.

Balefire: a fire lit for magical purposes, usually outdoors.

Casting a circle: the process of drawing a circle around oneself to seal out unfriendly influences and raise magical power. It is the first step in a spell.

Censer: an incense burner. Traditionally, a censer is a metal container, filled with incense, that is swung on the end of a chain.

Censing: the process of burning incense to spiritually cleanse an object.

Centering yourself: to prepare for a magical rite by calming and centering all of your personal energy.

Chakra: one of the seven centers of spiritual energy in the human body, according to the philosophy of yoga.

Charging: to infuse an object with magical power.

Circle of protection: a circle cast to protect oneself from unfriendly influences.

Crystals: quartz or other stones that store cleansing or protective energies.

Deosil: clockwise movement, symbolic of life and positive energies.

Deva: a divine being according to Hindu beliefs; a devil or evil spirit according to Zoroastrianism.

Direct/Retrograde: refers to the motions of the planets when seen from the Earth. A planet is "direct" when it appears to be moving forward from the point of view of a person on the Earth. It is "retrograde" when it appears to be moving backward.

Dowsing: to use a divining rod to search for a thing, usually water or minerals.

Dowsing pendulum: a long cord with a coin or gem at one end. The pattern of its swing is used to predict the future.

Dryad: a tree spirit or forest guardian.

Fey: an archaic term for a magical spirit or a fairylike being.

Gris-gris: a small bag containing charms, herbs, stones, and other items to draw energy, luck, love, or prosperity to the wearer.

Mantra: a sacred chant used in Hindu tradition to embody the divinity invoked; it is said to possess deep magical power.

Needfire: a ceremonial fire kindled at dawn on major Wiccan holidays. It was traditionally used to light all other household fires.

Pentagram: a symbolically protective five-pointed star with one point upward.

Power hand: the dominant hand, the hand used most often.

Scry: to predict the future by gazing at or into an object such as a crystal ball or pool of water.

Second sight: the psychic power or ability to foresee the future.

Sigil: a personal seal or symbol.

Smudge/Smudge stick: to spiritually cleanse an object by waving incense over and around it. A smudge stick is a bundle of several incense sticks.

Wand: a stick or rod used for casting circles and as a focus for magical power.

Widdershins: counterclockwise movement, symbolic of negative magical purposes, sometimes used to disperse negative energies.

Spell–A–Day Icons

 New Moon

 Money, Prosperity

 Full Moon

 Protection

 Abundance

 Relationship

 Altar

 Success

 Balance

 Travel, Communication

 Clearing, Cleaning

 Air Element

 Garden

 Earth Element

 Grab Bag

 Fire Element

 Health

 Spirit Element

 Home

 Water Element

 Heart, Love

 Meditation, Divination

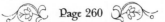

Spell Notes:

Spell Notes:

Spell Notes:

Spell Notes: